Leatherwork and Tanning

Leatherwork and Tanning

by
Lynn Huggins-Cooper

PEN & SWORD
HISTORY

AN IMPRINT OF PEN & SWORD BOOKS LTD.
YORKSHIRE – PHILADELPHIA

First published in Great Britain in 2018 by
Pen & Sword History
An imprint of
Pen & Sword Books Ltd
Yorkshire – Philadelphia

ISBN 978 1 52672 448 9

A CIP catalogue record for this book is
available from the British Library.

Printed and bound in England by TJ International Ltd, Padstow, Cornwall

Pen & Sword Books Limited incorporates the imprints of Atlas, Archaeology,
Aviation, Discovery, Family History, Fiction, History, Maritime, Military,
Military Classics, Politics, Select, Transport, True Crime, Air World, Frontline
Publishing, Leo Cooper, Remember When, Seaforth Publishing, The Praetorian
Press, Wharncliffe Local History, Wharncliffe Transport, Wharncliffe True
Crime and White Owl.

For a complete list of Pen & Sword titles please contact

PEN & SWORD BOOKS LIMITED
47 Church Street, Barnsley, South Yorkshire, S70 2AS, England
E-mail: enquiries@pen-and-sword.co.uk
Website: www.pen-and-sword.co.uk

Or
PEN AND SWORD BOOKS
1950 Lawrence Rd, Havertown, PA 19083, USA
E-mail: Uspen-and-sword@casematepublishers.com
Website: www.penandswordbooks.com

Contents

Introduction to Heritage Crafts

Heritage crafts are a part of what makes us who we are; part of the glue that has held families and communities together for centuries. That jumper your nanna knitted? A heritage craft. The willow basket made by your auntie? A heritage craft. Grandpa's hand turned pipe? Again, a heritage craft. These traditional crafts have been carried out for centuries, often handed down through families with a child learning the craft at a parent's knee. Heritage crafts are those traditional crafts that are a part of the customs and cultural heritage of the areas where they begin. A heritage craft is:

'a practice which employs manual dexterity and skill and an understanding of traditional materials, design and techniques, and which has been practised for two or more successive generations'.

Radcliffe Red List of Endangered Crafts Report, Heritage Crafts Association 2017

Heritage crafts are in trouble. The Heritage Crafts Association commissioned research into endangered crafts, supported by The Radcliffe Trust (http://theradcliffetrust.org/). The results make sobering reading. Greta Bertram, Secretary of the Heritage Crafts Association who led the research said:

'The Radcliffe Red List of Endangered Crafts is the first research of its kind in the UK. We're all familiar with the idea of a red list of

endangered species, but this is the first time the methodology has been applied to our intangible craft heritage. While some crafts are indeed thriving, the research has shown that all crafts, and not just those identified as critically endangered, face a wide range of challenges to their long-term survival. When any craft is down to the last few makers it has to be considered at risk as an unpredicted twist of fate can come at any time.'

Some of the heritage crafts identified in the report are teetering on the brink of disaster, and could be lost during this generation. One hundred and sixty-nine crafts were surveyed and allocated a status of currently viable, endangered, critically endangered or extinct. The survey team spoke to craft organisations and craftspeople, heritage professionals and funding bodies, as well as members of the public.

Four crafts surveyed were seen as already extinct, having been lost in the last ten years: riddle and sieve making, cricket ball making, gold beating and lacrosse stick making.

Ian Keys, Chair of the Heritage Crafts Association, said:

'We would like to see the Government recognise the importance of traditional craft skills as part of our cultural heritage, and take action to ensure they are passed on to the next generation. Craft skills today are in the same position that historic buildings were a hundred years ago – but we now recognise the importance of old buildings as part of our heritage, and it's time for us to join the rest of the world and recognise that these living cultural traditions are just as important and need safeguarding too.'

An alarming seventeen more crafts are seen by the report as critically endangered and at serious risk. There are few artisans practising the crafts – sometimes there are just one or two businesses operating – and there are few or no trainees learning the craft anew as apprentices. So why do we find ourselves in this situation? At a time when a huge variety of crafts enjoyed as a hobby is booming and craft fairs pop up in every community centre, village hall and historic estate, it seems odd that traditional crafts are dying out. So why is there a problem?

The study found that for some of the endangered crafts, there was an ageing workforce with nobody young training, waiting in the wings to take over. For others, there were found to be few training courses, even if there were potential trainees. For some traditional crafters the problem was found to be a variety of economic factors. Cheap competing crafts from overseas have flooded the market and there is often an unwillingness on the part of the public to pay a fair price for items handmade in Britain, despite the craftsmanship involved and the high quality of products. Of course, most traditional craftspeople are running micro-businesses and it is increasingly difficult to run a small business in Britain with an increase in paperwork, red tape, rules and regulations. Add to this the quantity of bureaucratic tasks and marketing necessary for self-employment and that leaves scant time for honing and practising an artisanal craft.

Three crafts that are part of the leather making and tanning industry have been identified as critically endangered: tanning with oak bark, parchment and vellum making, and collar making for heavy horses and harness driving. 'Critical' status means, according to the study, that there is a shrinking number of craftspeople carrying out the craft and that there are limited training opportunities for those wanting to enter the craft. It means that entering the craft has limited financial viability. Today, for example, oak bark tanning by hand on an industrial scale is only carried out by one producer in Britain: J. and F.J. Baker and Co. Ltd in Devon. Despite producing finer, stronger leather than chemical production, such as chrome tanning, this mode of production is expensive due to the time taken and is only used for high-end products; rightly so, as the process of tanning is a slow, meditative process. The bark itself is dried for two to three years before being crushed for use and the entire process of oak bark tanning may take up to fourteen months.

The future of heritage crafts is threatened in Great Britain. Action needs to be taken now to reverse the trend and ensure that these heritage cultural traditions are not lost forever. So far, we are failing. Great Britain is one of only twenty-two countries out of 194 to not have ratified the 2003 UNESCO Convention on the Safeguarding of Intangible Cultural Heritage. This convention focuses on the non-physical aspects of heritage such as traditional festivals, oral traditions, performing arts and the knowledge and skills to produce traditional crafts. If governmental action is not taken soon, many heritage crafts will be consigned to history.

You can help by supporting heritage craftworkers with your wallet and by attending demonstrations and events. You can also join the Heritage Crafts Association, even if you are not a heritage crafter yourself, to support the funding and research of heritage craft practices. At the time of writing, in 2017, it is £20 for an individual to join. (http://heritagecrafts. org.uk/get-involved/)

Introduction to Leatherwork and Tanning

The supple feel of a leather jacket, the spicy scent of leather boots and the glow of dubbin – leather has a sensual appeal all of its own. Tanning and leatherworking have been a part of everyday human life since prehistoric times. Before plastic, rubber, silicone and other flexible and waterproof materials, skins were a vital part of life. Hides, and then later processed leather, were the go-to materials for clothing, shelter and more. This was due to the material's durability, strength, flexibility and waterproofing. Hide has always been readily available as a by-product when animals are slaughtered for food; it is pliable, strong and when it is tanned, it is waterproof. The fact that it has endured as a key material throughout human history – even into the modern age, when we have access to such a multiplicity of materials, with new substances invented every year – attests to its importance and popularity.

Depending on the type of animal the original skin comes from and the way in which it is treated, leather can be soft and supple like fabric or rigid and strong like wood. The key to a skin's properties as potential leather is the amount of collagen it contains. It is the collagen fibres that makes skin (even human skin) flexible and strong. Leather can be made from the skin of most vertebrates, yet the same species of animals have been chosen more regularly: cow, pig, goat, sheep, horse and deer. This choice is often tied in to the types of animals slaughtered for meat, as those skins are left as a by-product of butchery and consumption. Cultural values also play a part, as well as practicality with regard to the area of usable leather a skin can provide. Exotic leathers such as crocodile, seal, reptile and snake skin, and sometimes types of fish skin have also been used for their beauty and decorative value as well as their strength. Historically, sometimes even dog and cat skins were used to make leather items.

As leather is an organic material, archaeologists face major challenges in the excavation of leather items and goods. Many examples of historic leatherwork have been lost to rotting and decay and it only really survives in special conditions – for example, waterlogged and safe from the air in bog land, or sealed into dry, cold excavation sites such as caves. Add to this the further complication that much of the historic leather that is excavated has been subject to conditions that can change its composition. Salt water played a part in the case of leather found on the Tudor ship, *The Mary Rose* and the *Metta Catharina*, sunk in 1786, making it difficult to assess tanning processes used. Bog conditions complicated the situation in the case of the Tollund Man, found on the Jutland peninsula in Denmark and the Elling Woman found west of Silkeborg in Denmark. Plant material natural to the peat bog contained tannins of its own, complicating the study of tanning methods used on the worked leather the bodies were wearing. This means it can be hard to decipher the 'evidence' in many cases – it may, for example, make leather seem to have been tanned in a certain way when in fact the 'tanning' has occurred as a result of the natural conditions in the location where the find was made.

Despite these challenges, thousands of examples of leatherwork from the Roman, Viking, Medieval and later periods have been found by archaeologists, which of course attests to the frequency with which leather as a material was used. It was ubiquitous, being used for clothing, shoes, for bags and pouches, sheathes for knives, parchment and vellum, protective clothing and horse harness. Some examples are so well preserved that we now know how historic stitching, cutting and shaping was done and how the leather was worked for decorative purposes. Leather was incised with patterns, engraved with blunt tools to mark the surface and even dyed and painted. Openwork – cutting small holes through the leather – can be seen in many Roman shoes. Our ancestors even gilded leather.

Like most technology, tanning is likely to have developed in response to a human problem or need. We are by nature problem solvers and the use and preservation of skins and hides would have made life warmer, safer and more comfortable for the earliest humans. Imagine, for example, how impossible it would have been to survive the Ice Age without the development of flint tools to kill and skin animals and to scrape the hides to make warm wraps, blankets, foot coverings and shelters.

Leather can, of course, be made from any type of animal skin – but in fact only skin that has been vegetable tanned or chemically tawed with mineral salts or alum should in fact be called 'leather'. Treating skins with fats, offal or smoke is technically speaking *pseudo tanning* rather than tanning. It cures the skins and makes them slower to rot, but does not make them water resistant in the same way as 'true' leather that has been tanned. Cured leather, such as chamois which is not tanned but is treated with oils and fats, will start to decay readily in damp conditions, for example.

True tanning happens when skins are immersed in water along with steeped vegetable matter, such as bark, galls and roots. The tannins are absorbed by the wet skins and leather is made. Simply put, a tannin is a molecule that bonds with the protein – collagen – in the skins and forces out water, taking its place. This preserves it and makes it water resistant. Have you ever drunk dark, heavy red wine and then felt that strange drying sensation, despite the fact that you are drinking liquid? That is as a result of the rich, oaky tannins in the wine, that come from the skin of the red grape.

Tannin is famously found in tea, but over the course of thousands of years, tanners identified the trees and plants in their locale that contained the high quantities of tannins for leather making. In England, bark oak was commonly used and readily available. In large areas of mainland Europe, chestnut was more common. In Russia, birch and willow were used and in America, hemlock and oak. Modern leather is also treated with a great many other materials and chemicals, as well as dye, to make it durable and colourful.

Imagine for a moment that you are living in the ancient world. You hang up skins in the rafters of your shelter to dry and you notice that the thick smoke from your fire helps preserve them. You realise that salting food preserves it, so perhaps it could help to preserve your animal hides. You might even have discovered alum tanning, by seeing what mineral deposits did to skins in volcanic areas of the world. Over time, these ancient methods developed and became more sophisticated.

Leathercraft and tanning methods are mentioned in ancient texts from Assyrian writing, in accounts of Roman life, in ancient Egyptian texts and even in Homer's Iliad. According to Homer, writing in the eighth century BC, Odysseus was rather romantically given a leather bag *full of storm winds* to help his ship make the journey to Ithaca.

In Mesopotamia, between the third and fifth centuries BC, archaeological evidence tells us that the Sumerians used leather to make gorgeous long, soft leather dresses and diadems for women. Assyrians used leather to make footwear and shoes, as well as containers and bottles for liquids and as ingenious flotation devices to keep rafts afloat. They produced the first examples of the fine skins we call 'Morocco' leather today. Phoenicians used leather for footwear and wearable items and, according to the historian Strabo, to create a complex system of water piping to create a water supply.

The ancient Egyptians used leather widely for items of clothing such as gloves and shoes, and the ancient Romans used leather across the empire. The earliest religious communities of monks were skilled at leathercraft and used it for shoes, bookbinding and the creation of vellum and parchment for manuscripts. Indeed, leather appears in some form in all civilisations throughout history.

Chapter 1

Ancient Leatherwork

From earliest times, people have used animal hides for clothing, bedding and containers for carrying things. Boats and shelters were made from leather and hides and cave paintings from Lerida in Spain show figures clad in animal hide. The earliest use of hides would likely have been by bands of hunters in the Paleolithic era and they would have been liable to have first used furs and skins in their raw, dried forms.

The skins and hides that these early hunters used would regularly stiffen or rot, so it makes sense that over time they would have developed ways to make the hides longer-lasting and more durable. The earliest methods of treating skins were a response to this need to make skins and hides more flexible and to protect against decay. Perhaps these hunters first stretched hides to dry and noticed that the smoke from their fires helped over time to preserve the skins. Maybe they also saw the result of a 'happy accident', where skins lying where they were affected by fallen leaves or plant material in puddles caused them to be preserved for longer. It is possible that by trying to make skins more flexible, they found that skin rot could also be slowed by treating the skins with other animal products such as fat and brains or other offal. All of this is, of course, speculation and the result of looking back in time with modern eyes to guess at the way in which the process of tanning developed. We will never know for sure, but it makes sense that by noticing things that helped to make skins last longer, they would start to use these methods to cure the hides as a matter of course.

It is safe to assume that trial and error and experimentation will have shaped the way that early people worked leather. It is testimony to the ingenuity of these early leather dressers that some of their methods – scraping the skins for example, to remove scraps of flesh and stretching skins on racks to dry – are still used today.

Recently, evidence has been found to suggest that even the Neanderthals, the very first, earliest people, used tools to dress and process leather. They used knapped flint knives and scrapers, and bone tools called *lissoir* which were discovered at dig sites in southwest France in caves at Abri Peyrony and Pech de l'Azé. It is thought that these deer bone tools were used to smooth and burnish leather by rubbing and buffing against the surface of the skin. When the bone was radio-carbon dated, it was found to be an incredible 51,000 years old. Lissoir type tools are still used for hand processing leather today, with their design virtually unchanged after more than 50,000 years. We have as a people been tanning skins to produce leather for a very long time indeed.

We know from excavated evidence that by Neolithic times, when people were beginning to farm animals, there was a steady source of skins that did not rely on the vagaries of hunting. We know from bone and stone tools found at digs that this was when they began to create quantities of *pseudo* leather, using animal by-products to treat and join the hides together. They probably scraped off the hair and rubbed the leather with brains and urine to make it pliable and soft. This economical hide dressing process would stay the same for thousands of years. Different cultures used different treatments, finally developing methods of true tanning of leather with different methods and ingredients from tree bark to pigeon faeces, lime and animal fat.

In 2008 the oldest leather shoe found to date was discovered by Diana Zardaryan, a postgraduate student on an archaeological dig in Armenia. It was 5,500 years old. It has been named the *Areni-1* shoe, after the Areni cave complex where it was found. The shoe was well preserved due to the cool, dry conditions in the caves – and a thick layer of sheep dung that had sealed over the shoe and other objects on the floor of the cave. The shoe was made in one piece, with surviving laces, and is similar to shoe designs found across Europe. When this stunning find was carbon dated, it was found to date back to 3500BC, making it a thousand years older than the shoes found at the Great Pyramid of Ghiza.

Otzi the Iceman was another great archaeological find, especially with regard to the history of leatherworking. This 5,300 year old mummy was discovered in 1991, by two German tourists walking in the Otztal Alps between Italy and Austria. At first, they believed they had found the frozen remains of a fallen climber – but after examination, the body turned out to be the oldest European mummified human remains. The body had been covered with ice soon after death so had frozen and was very well preserved.

The mummy's clothes were also well preserved. They included a loincloth, leggings, coat, shoes and belt – all made from leather. His snow-proof hat was made from bearskin with a leather chin strap. His shoes were also made specially for the snow, with waterproof deer hide tops and bearskin soles.

Otzi's coat, leggings, belt and loincloth were all made from vertical strips of leather, stitched together with sinew. His coat contained pieces of goatskin and sheepskin. His leggings were made from soft, flexible goatskin. His shoelaces were made from cattle hide and his arrow quiver was made from deerskin. His belt had a pouch attached which contained tools, including an awl and dried fungus, possibly for lighting a fire. His discovery gave archaeologists a window into early leatherwork.

Other fascinating discoveries about ancient leatherwork have been made as the result of a series of archaeological finds dubbed 'bog bodies', such as the *Tollund Man* and the *Elling Woman*. The acid nature of the peat in the bogs, along with a lack of oxygen under the surface and cool temperatures, preserved the soft tissues of the body, as well as much of the clothing.

The Elling Woman was found in a peat bog in Denmark in 1938, by farmer Jens Zakariasson. At first, he thought the body was in fact a drowned animal, but on examination it was found to be the remains of a woman, wrapped in a sheepskin cape, with a leather cloak wrapped around her legs. In 1976, the body was carbon dated and it was estimated that she had died around 280BC. Her cloak was stitched with fine thread, with delicate stitching. It had been repaired less skilfully in places with leather string. It is likely that the woman would have worn a cloak with fur inside, topped with the waterproof leather cloak, so she was kept both warm and dry.

The Tollund Man was found in the same bog by peat cutters in 1950. The body has been carbon dated to sometime between 375 and 210BC. Tollund Man was wearing a sheepskin leather and wool cap, fastened by a leather thong. He had a smooth hide belt round his waist and a hide noose round his neck. Once again, archaeologists learned a great deal about early leatherwork due to the excavations.

Leathercraft was developing around the globe in ancient times. In Egypt, leathercraft was sophisticated, fine and intricate. Leather was used for making shoes, bags, sheaths for daggers, animal collars, musical instruments and bracelets. It was also used for making furniture, harness and even chariots and shields. Specially prepared hide was used sometimes in place of papyrus as a writing surface. Beautiful stools upholstered with goatskin were found in the tomb of Tutankhamun.

The Egyptian Museum in Cairo houses the world's oldest leather manuscript. It dates from 2300-2000BC, and is an amazing 2.5 metres long. The religious manuscript contains depictions of supernatural and divine figures and is older than the famous 'Book of the Dead'.

Priests carried sacred texts written on leather rolls to use during ceremonies and rituals. The leather was regarded as precious, being more durable and flexible than papyrus, and was often used for sacred writings.

The museum also houses an incredible collection of leatherwork from an ancient chariot, including harnesses, gauntlets and a bow case. Yet the collection lay forgotten and hidden for many years in a store room. In 2008, ancient leatherwork expert Andre Veldmeijer from the Netherlands-Flemish Institute in Cairo saw photographs of chariot leatherwork in a book from the 1950s. He approached the curator of the museum, Ibrahim El Gawad, who did not know where the chariot pieces were kept. El Gawad identified the chariot in a catalogue and found them in store room drawers. The pieces were nearly complete and included the leather casing from the wooden chariot. The detailed patterning and decoration in red, white and green was still bright and the stitching was intact. Salima Ikram, from the American University in Cairo joined Veldmeijer to work on the chariot project and identified a strap that she thought worked as a safety belt. She has since discovered that the strap was some sort of collar or neck strap for the horse and that the reins were sometimes worn around the charioteers' hips or buttocks, to help control the horses. Veldmeijer is now working to identify the type of leather and the tanning methods used, as well as studying how the leather was cut and stitched.

But who did the chariot belong to? El Gawad thinks it may have been Akhenaten, Tutankhamun's father, but Veldmeijer thinks they may be from one of Tutankhamun's successors. It seems likely that the chariot dates from the late Eighteenth Dynasty (1549-1292 BC) or the early Nineteenth Dynasty (1292-1189 BC). As more is discovered about the chariot, we will learn about ancient Egyptian leathercraft and the technology used to create large leather pieces.

From 4BC chamois leather was tanned with fat and other leathers, such as skin from cows, sheep and goats, were tanned with vegetable matter such as acacia pods. Some leathers were coloured with a red dye made from scale insects and others were coloured yellow with dye made from the skins of pomegranates. In Assyria and Babylonia, evidence of tanning with alum, gall-nuts, sumach and myrrh have been found.

Vellum and parchment are materials made from skins that have been used for manuscripts, drawing, drum skins and making books for thousands of years. The earliest remaining evidence of writing on material made from skins is a fragment that dates back to the Sixth Dynasty in ancient Egypt – an astonishing 2400BC, now held by the Cairo Museum. The Greek historian Herodotus refers to writing on prepared skins in 500BC. The advantage these materials have over paper is that they remain flexible and are more hardwearing. There is a Fourth Century bible, the Codex Sinaiticus, that was written on vellum and can still be read today.

Vellum was made from calfskin and parchment was generally made from goatskin. The skin is prepared by soaking in water containing lime. The hair was removed from the skin by scraping with a double-handed knife called a scudder. The knife was drawn gently across the surface and the hair came away. The skins were stretched on a frame and the craftsperson scraped the skin to raise the grain and smooth the surface. The vellum was treated with pumice powder or chalk to help to make it a dry and smooth surface to write upon.

Leathercraft was carried out across the ancient world and travellers, traders and settlers took their practices, tools and methods with them, cross-pollinating the craft as they went. People have been riding horses for thousands of years and rode long distances to travel and trade. The first things we could identify as 'saddles' appeared over 4,000 years ago, but these were little more than cloth or hide pads. They would, however, have made the long journeys taken during migrations more comfortable.

By 700BC Assyrian warriors owned elaborate saddle cloths that included girth-like straps. These saddles were often used as status symbols, showing off the rider's wealth and position. Embellishments such as intricate stitching, precious metals and gilding and the addition of carved wood and horn were added.

An archaeological dig of a tomb in the Pazyryk region of Siberia, from 5BC discovered a beautifully decorated saddle cover made from felt and leather. The people from this culture were nomads and horse traders. The tombs were well preserved because they became waterlogged when water seeped into the tombs and froze solid. The tombs contained silk, carpets and elaborate equine equipment, as well as the horses themselves.

By the second century BC, stirrups emerged in India. A model of a rider using stirrups was found during the excavation of a Chinese tomb from around 302AD, and by 477AD its use was widespread in China, spreading then across the world.

The Romans used leather for footwear, clothing, armour, shields and harness. As the Roman Empire marched across the world, they took their technology and artisans with them and spread their tanning and leathercrafting processes across the globe.

Ancient Britons used leather for clothing and footwear, as well as making bags and covering early boats, known as coracles, in leather to make them waterproof. As successive waves of invaders and settlers came to the shores of Britain, they brought their ways of working leather with them.

Romans first came to Britain in 55BC when they invaded under the orders of Julius Caesar. Caesar's two invasions were not strictly speaking successful, but they did establish Britain as a trading partner for Rome. This brought an influx of Roman goods into Britain, including leatherwork. In 43AD the emperor Claudius conquered Britain and the long Roman occupation began.

The Romans were skilled leather makers. The rich archaeological evidence they left behind in the villas, forts and fortifications they built across Britain has left us with examples of their complex methods of working with skin, fur and sinew that affected the way that leather was processed forever, not just in the Roman empire, but throughout the world.

The Romans used leather in all areas of life, domestic and military. They used it for making items of clothing and footwear as well as in military applications, such as shield covers and backing for metal armour. They used leather to make harnesses and equine equipment; they used it for bags, flasks, purses and decorative objects. Contrary to some Hollywood suggestions, the Romans did not use leather routinely to create armour itself, however, even though it was used along with metal to make a more protective body covering for soldiers. As armour, leather proved useless when wet and knives could pass through it easily – as noted by Pliny the Elder in a discussion of hippopotamus hide as a protective device. It seems a shame really, as the image of soldiers clad in hippo-skin armour is a beguiling one...

Excavations at Vindolanda Roman fort in Northumberland have revealed the scale of leatherwork carried out by the occupying army. The collection of leather here, standing at around 6,600 items and rising, is the largest found anywhere in what was the Roman Empire. There are thousands of shoes, together with bags, purses, buckets and vessels and archery guards in the collection at Vindolanda. Of course, this valuable collection keeps on growing, as Vindolanda is a site that is still being excavated forty years after the first dig. It is one of the primary Roman era archaeological sites in Europe and still has a wealth of artefacts waiting to be discovered.

Think for a moment of the Roman soldiers, far from their homes around the world, stationed in Britain, on the Roman wall. It would have been cold and bleak for much of the year and it was a brutally exposed site with little protection from freezing weather fronts from the north. The importance of warm shelter would be massive to the soldiers first stationed there – quite literally, a matter of life or death from exposure and hypothermia. Digs have revealed portions of leather tents created by the Romans to keep out the cold and wet, being used perhaps when they were constructing new forts and settlements, travelling between one camp and another, when on campaign, or when on manoeuvres. Goatskin was sewn together to create the tents, using specially designed seams to ensure that water ran off rather than penetrated the tents. It has been estimated by archaeologists that around seventy skins were needed for each tent.

Much further south in London, a dig carried out in 2013 by the Museum of London Archaeology on the banks of the Thames revealed a huge cache of 250 Roman shoes – the largest set of Roman leatherwork ever found in London. The damp had preserved much of the leather in good condition, revealing details about the complexity of the leatherwork carried out at the time. The collection includes military shoes, such as *caliga*, as well as sandals and cork-soled shoes. There is evidence that the Romans sensibly recycled precious leather, as off cuts were found of leather sheet panels, probably taken from defunct tents and shelters, that had been trimmed away from seams to make footwear.

Most Roman era leather was made from goat and cow hide. It is widely believed that the Romans introduced the vegetable tanning of hides to northern Europe, so that the first 'true' leather (rather than the previously cured hides treated with animal products or smoke) was first introduced to Britain by these fierce invaders. The fact that Roman leatherwork remains are 'true' leather means they have been more likely to survive the centuries, and it's a testimony to these early tanning techniques that we have so many amazing finds. Leather was a commonly used material in the Roman era and that has meant that we are fortunate to have many examples, often excavated from ditches and wells. Most of the leather that archaeologists have found from this period of history comes from forts occupied for many years. As with any area of human occupation, rubbish would pile up and need to be dealt with; the rubbish that was put into pits then, is story-filled treasure in the modern day, as it tells us so much about the Roman way of life.

The Romans used millions of hides, both in civilian and military life. Fascinating information recorded on tablets found at Vindolanda in Northumberland shows us that hides formed part of the trade that Romans carried out in Britain. Skins were probably sent from across the empire as trade, including goat skins from north Africa, for example, as there may have been a short supply in Britain and goat skins were a mainstay of Roman leatherwork. Records show that the Romans often used taxation payable in goods from the provinces and used it to gather essential supplies, and this included hides. It is possible that these would then be gathered centrally to be tanned by the Romans, for their military needs. There is evidence of a great tannery at Pompeii, for example, in the excavations that have occurred of the area swamped by lava when Vesuvius erupted in 79AD. Elsewhere, evidence of centralised tanning has been somewhat harder to find. It has been suggested that this might be because tannery equipment is so unremarkable – racks, pits, frames – that the tanneries have not been recognised, as the equipment and tools could have had a myriad of purposes.

Roman methods of tanning were labour intensive, and it took some considerable time to turn skin and hides to leather. Needing time for the process means that anywhere that was not a permanent base – or was perhaps a less secure military base, in a besieged area – would be no good for tanning purposes, as any hides that were half tanned would be rendered useless. The Romans in occupation often moved regularly as orders were sent from Rome for new fortifications and occupation. This could make tanning operations impossible, once again suggesting the need for a more centralised method of leather tanning and production.

Some sites have yielded evidence of leatherworking on a grand scale, such as at Carlisle. The excavation of the fort and *vicus*, or nearby civilian camp, revealed nearly 2,500 items of leatherworking waste, such as discarded tent seams, where leather was recycled into other items, or waste leather. Archaeologists also refer to something they call the 'proxy record' as evidence for a given practice taking place. Tools that *could* be used for leather making but also other activities would come under this type of evidence for leather making and leathercraft. There was a great deal of this proxy evidence present at the Carlisle digs.

At Vindolanda, a report lists twelve shoemakers, or *sutores*, who were employed as leatherwork artisans to make footwear for the military. *Tabernacularius* – tent-makers – were also employed there. Whether hides were gathered locally via taxation, or sent from far flung parts of the empire in trade, a great deal were needed by the Romans provisioning their military forces on the wall at Vindolanda.

In 408AD, the Romans finally left Britain. This left the country open to waves of invaders and settlers who continued to arrive on the shores, including Angles, Saxons and Jutes from Scandinavia and northern Germany. These people left their mark on the way society and trades worked, including the leathercrafting practices used in Britain. The tanning processes used by these Anglo Saxons would remain largely the same until the seventeenth century.

During the Anglo-Saxon period, leather was used to make a huge variety of everyday objects. Shoes, belts, hoods, cloaks and jerkins were made from hide, and garments were sometimes coated with fish oils to make them waterproof – a rather pungent form of treatment for clothing! Useful items such as pouches, bags and bottles were made from leather as it was hardwearing and flexible. Saddles, bridles and ropes were also made from leather, as were knife scabbards and shield covers.

The Anglo Saxons processed hides meticulously. Once the animal was skinned, they removed any remaining flesh or fat with scrapers, soaking the hide to make the job easier. If it was a skin with hair, it was soaked in a solution of ash, urine or quicklime. This made the hair loosen and the pores of the skin open so it was easier to remove the hair with a scraper. After this treatment, the skin would have become a kind of rawhide. Some of these skins were soaked in a stinking solution of chicken and pigeon droppings and dog faeces. This neutralised the lime, while the bacteria in the solution opened the pores in the skin more and 'bated' the leather. The more the leather was bated, the more flexible and useful it became.

After this treatment, the leather was soaked in vats of urine, where the ammonia removed more of the alkalinity of the lime. Then the skins were soaked in a liquor made from water and crushed oak bark, so the tannin would seep deeply into the structure of the skin. Willow, alder and elm bark was also sometimes used, depending on what was available in the locale. The tannin provided by the plant material creates 'true leather' by preserving the skin and forcing out moisture. This allows the finished leather to become heat and waterproof and guards against rotting. This whole intricate process could take more than a year to complete. Once the leather was tanned and ready, it was scrubbed and dried on a rack, before being finished with fish oil. This oil was rubbed on with a wad of sheepskin so that it penetrated the surface of the leather and helped to make it pliable. Then a skilled *currier* finished the leather, polishing it with bone tools and adding more oil. The leather may also have been dyed with plant dyes and then polished again with fat such as tallow.

Finally, the leather would be ready to cut and stitch. Sharp knives were used to cut the leather to shape, and holes were made with needles and awls, ready for it to be stitched together. Sometimes the leather would also be decorated. It might be painted or worked with tools. The surface was sometimes dampened and a design stamped or engraved with metal, wood or bone tools.

After an awl, or a sharp point, was used to make the holes ready for the needle to be passed through, strong wool, gut or waxed linen thread would be used to join the pieces together. Due to the properties and texture of the leather, the hole made by the awl would close again around the thread after stitching, making a strong join.

In 793 the Vikings arrived. The invasion of monasteries such as the community at Lindisfarne, on the north-eastern coast of Britain, gave the marauding Vikings access to gold and riches. They, of course, brought with them their own leather-worked items, in the form of shoes, belts, scabbards and pouches. Leather would have been a useful material to the seafaring and warlike Vikings, as it was waterproof and tough, rather like the warriors who wore it. Archaeologists have found evidence of leatherworkshops during excavations of Viking-era towns, as well as many examples of excavated leather items.

The Vikings would continue to raid the coasts of Britain until the eleventh century, when they started to settle and colonise parts of the country, having families with members of the local population. York, known in the Viking era as *Jorvik*, has yielded a great deal of evidence of leatherworking, especially around the Coppergate area. Evidence has been found of shoe making and caches of leather finds have included the remains of straps, belts and finely decorated scabbards and sheaths. Offcuts from cattle and sheep leather were also found, showing archaeologists where leatherworking took place. Tools were also found, including knives, punches, creasers and awls, needles and beeswax, all of which are commensurate with the leatherworking industry. Evidence was also found of dyeing leather and cloth with plant materials such as woad and green-weed. Archaeologists have also found the remains of treatment with ash which was used in the dyeing process. There was evidence to support the disposal of waste from dye baths, which could have been used for dyeing leather items as well as cloth and wool.

Due to the plethora of Viking-era leather finds, we have a good idea of the type of leather objects made during this period. Leather caps have been found, as have wrap round ankle-length boots and shoes. Shoes were usually made in a 'turn-shoe' style, which means they were sewn, then turned inside-out so the seam was on the inside of the shoe. The holes from the sewing were then on the inside, so the shoe was potentially less likely to let in water. Shoes wore out quickly, so they were discarded on rubbish heaps which is why archaeologists have found many examples. Women's shoes were similar in style to men's shoes. Leather was also used to make belts and, as clothing had no pockets, a leather pouch was worn on the belt to hold coins, fire-starting kits etc.

Animal skins and furs were used for warmth and durability in clothing. There was an extensive Viking fur trade and remnants of squirrel, beaver, bear, fox and pine marten have been excavated at Birka, an old Viking trading town. Reference is made in the *Fóstbrœðra Saga* (the Sagas of Icelanders which were based on events taking place in the ninth, tenth and early eleventh centuries) to a seal skin coat and trousers. The *Bárðar saga Snæfellsás* describes a great fur cloak. Some types of fur, such as bear skin, were worn as status symbols showing that the wearer was 'brave' enough to hunt a bear.

So, in ancient times, leather was a precious commodity. It was made around the globe, with strikingly similar techniques. This may of course have been due to migration, trade routes and the influence of invaders who brought their leather technology with them. It could be highly decorated and tooled, or plain and simple – but in an often harsh world it could mean the difference between life and death in terms of shelter, clothing and footwear.

Chapter 2

Medieval Leathercraft

The leather industry was an important part of medieval life and trade. The versatile material was used to make wearable items such as shoes, gloves and bags. It was also used to make equine equipment such as harness and saddles. By the Middle Ages, saddles had to be strong and supportive to carry the weight of armour. They were built on a wooden tree, padded with wool and horse hair and covered with leather. Military items such as scabbards for swords and knives and even types of armour were also made from leather.

Contemporary records stated that:

'In most villages in the realm there is someone, dresser or worker of leather, and for the supplies of such as have not, there are in most market towns three, four or five and in many great towns and cities ten and twenty, and in London and its suburbs nearly two hundred.'

Cherry, J. (1991, 301) 'Leather', in Blair et al English Medieval Industries: Craftsmen, techniques, products

Medieval place names from the period, that remain to this day in many towns and cities also tell us that tanneries were widespread; for example, *Tanner Row* and *Barker Row* dating from the medieval era in York, and *Tanner Street* in Northampton.

Rules were laid down by law in this period governing which artisans in the leather industry could take part in the different aspects of the process of making leather goods. Tanners, for example, were not allowed to work as butchers. Curriers were not permitted to do the work of tanners. Curriers were not allowed to work as cordwainers, and so on. Rules were strict, and thorough. In 1184, for example, orders were given that no tanner or tawyer (workers who processed 'small' skins) could set up or practise trade within the bounds of a forest, except in a market town or borough. This was to stop the poaching of deer for their skins. In 1351, a series of regulations and rules at a parliamentary and municipal level separated off the two industries of tanning, currying, tawing and leatherworking. This separation was supposed to reduce the likelihood of any sort of monopoly occurring in the leather industry.

Monastic houses often maintained their own tanneries in the medieval period, producing leather for everything from footwear to book binding. Meaux Abbey, a large Cistercian monastery near Beverley in the East Riding of Yorkshire, ran a tannery. In 1396, an inventory showed that they held a variety of calf leather, and cow hide, in 'sole peces, sclepe, clowthedys, and wambes' worth £14 10s 4d. It also detailed fifteen tubs and various tools such as three 'schapyng-knyfes'. It also held 400 tan turves, the blocks of bark the tannins were derived from. This was a large amount, which perhaps reveals the quantity of leather being tanned in the monastery at the time.

Monasteries were also great producers – and users – of parchment and vellum. In medieval times, the parchment maker was called a percamenarius or parchmenter. These artisans would be found in every town in the country, providing writing material for scribes and book sellers for manuscripts, books and prayers for religious houses. They would choose the best unblemished skins to make parchment for a smooth finish that was pleasant to write upon and illuminate. White beasts would produce the palest, luxurious parchment. Once the skin had been soaked in lime water to remove hair, it would be attached to a frame to dry. The skin was attached with strings held by pegs, to allow for the skin to shrink as it dried. The pegs would be turned to tighten and stretch the skin which had to be done slowly and carefully. Any nicks or cuts in the skin would open during stretching, producing holes in the drying material. The *parchmenter* would scrape the skin with a curved knife called a *lunellum*. Once the skin was dried, it would be scraped again, with the craftworker trying to create a uniform thickness. Early parchment and vellum was quite thick, but by the thirteenth century techniques allowed for a thinner, delicately textured finish. Once finished, the vellum or parchment was rolled up and sold in sheets. Historically, vellum was difficult to use as the surface was often greasy, despite its treatment. Writers used a compound called *pounce* to dust the vellum prior to use. This was made from crushed pumice stone or cuttlefish bone. Sometimes thin pastes were rubbed into the skins to make them whiter, using lime, egg white, flour and milk. Some writers improvised and used materials such as crushed eggshell, alum, resin or powdered incense. This paste was called *staunchgrain*.

In *Il Libro del Arte*, written in the fifteenth century, Cennini provided recipes for material to tint parchment green, indigo, peach and purple. Examples of books using purple vellum still can be seen in museums today, such as the sixth century Rossano Gospels, written in silver ink. Interestingly, in the seventh to ninth centuries, as parchment and vellum were so expensive, they were often re-used. The writing was scrubbed or scoured away, and this sometimes left behind ghosting of earlier texts. Recycled parchment used in this way is called a palimpsest. Who can tell what valuable writings were lost in this way?

Parchment and vellum are made by one company in the UK today – William Cowley in Buckinghamshire. Being made from collagen, the skin has an unusual quality that is still valued by some artists in the modern day. When water (or paint mixed in water) touches the surface of the collagen it raises and becomes pliable, creating an interesting effect and finish.

Tanning as an industry expanded rapidly in the medieval period. Skins were readily available as a by-product of the butchery trade in market towns in particular. The butchers were compelled to bring the hides of the creatures they butchered for meat into the market, along with the meat itself, and tanners had the sole right to buy the skins. Butchers and skinners would flay the skins, and tanners and fellmongers would buy them. Only tanners were permitted to buy cow hide. Fellmongers, who were hide merchants, prepared other skins for sale by trimming and washing them, and removing hair. They could buy skins such as goat, sheep, deer and pig skins. Tawers and whittawers prepared these smaller animal skins ready for use. They used a solution of potash alum and salt, together with egg and flour to process the skins. This did not make 'true' leather, and was not waterproof, but it was a useful material in the medieval world.

Evidence has been excavated that tells us that tanning pits were used in the medieval period and inner horn waste (after the outer hard keratinous part of the horn has been removed and sold for use elsewhere) has been found nearby – always a good indicator of tanning activity in a location. Hooves and horns were left attached to the skins by the butcher as they had no worth in meat terms, so they were usually removed by tanners; hence the waste being identified as an indicator of tanning activity. The hide would then be washed, usually in the town stream – and this was very polluting, as dung, blood and mud was washed away in the same water that supplied the town's drinking supply. There were regular complaints about this water fouling activity carried out by tanneries in the production of leather. In 1306, tanners were held partially responsible for the fouling and subsequent blockage of the course of the River Fleet in London, and in 1461 complaints were recorded when one William

Frankwell reserved the right to use a ditch at the side of his meadow for tanning, as it threatened to pollute the town water supplies.

Tanning was an important and lucrative business in the Middle Ages, and like the cloth industry, it attracted a high degree of control by town authorities as well as at a governmental level. It was 'big business' and open to abusive and fraudulent practices. Tanned leather was regularly examined by 'searchers', officials either appointed by the town authorities or the craft guild themselves. This kept tanning standards high. Once inspected, leather would be stamped with the searcher's own seal, which marked it as genuine, well-tanned leather of a good quality. This inspection could happen at market, or in the 'seld' – the craft hall where leather was sold.

After hides were washed, the next step was the removal of scraps of flesh, fat and hair that still adhered to the hide. This was achieved by immersing the skins in a lime pit or by soaking in urine. Some evidence suggests the rather pungent and unsavoury – yet efficient – practice of skins being dowsed with urine and left in the sun to become slightly putrescent so that the pores on the skin opened, making the hair easier to remove. Once the hair loosened, it would be scraped off with a blunt knife, and any flesh and fat would be removed with a sharper double-bladed knife. The hide would then be immersed in a solution made with warmed dog or bird faeces, or dunked in a solution of barley, rye, beer or urine. These processes would neutralise the alkalinity of the lime and make the leather softer in the process.

Finally, the prepared skins would be soaked in the tanning pits, in a solution of water and crushed oak bark. This solution was rather colourfully referred to as 'wooses' – which it has been suggested by historians as a derivative of 'oozes'. Oak bark for tanning was gathered between April and June when the sap was rising and it was easiest to peel. It was then dried after gathering and ground at bark mills by huge millstones powered by water or animal power. There is evidence of a bark mill at Marley, at Battle Abbey in East Sussex. Once in the pits, the skins would be moved from time to time to ensure an equal coverage of colour in the leather. The skins would remain in the pits for around a year. After removal from the pit, the skin would be rinsed and smoothed before being put in sheds to dry slowly. When they were dry, the currier could take over and finish the skins.

Curriers dressed and finished the leather, after it had been processed at the tannery, using a combination of oils and fats. They also sometimes dyed the leather. Currying helped to make the leather stronger, more flexible and water resistant. Curriers also stretched the leather on racks and burnished it to a fine finish. Sometimes the skins would be dampened again and trampled or pummelled to soften them. They would then be brushed or smoothed with stones. Skins would also be stretched on racks and shaved to obtain a uniform thickness, rinsed again, then rubbed with greases such as tallow and fish oils. The skins would be piled up to ensure that these greases and oils penetrated evenly and then the hides would be hung to dry and any excess grease cleaned away. If a finer leather was required, with a high degree of suppleness, it would be 'boarded', or rubbed on a flat surface such as a table. At this stage, the leather could be coloured and polished. When the currier finished these processes, the leather was finally ready to be sold to leatherworkers.

Further inspection by 'searchers' could take place in some towns at the currier's workshop to check for quality. Curriers were not even allowed to dress hides deemed to be poor quality or badly tanned. In London in 1378, searchers examined forty-seven hides being held for currying, belonging to one Nicholas Burle. They were found to be poor quality and badly tanned. He admitted that they were not fine enough quality for shoe making, but claimed that they were intended for sale to saddlers and leather bottle makers, who required a lesser quality of leather. However, a mixed jury of his peers in these trades decided that the leather was so bad it was unfit for any purpose and the leather was confiscated.

If the skins were bought from the butcher or fellmonger by a tawyer or whittawyer, rather than a tanner, the process used was different. The skins (sheep, goat, deer, horse, dog – no cow hides as these were exclusively available to tanners) were cleaned in a similar way to those used by tanners, and were then steeped in a paste made from alum, flour, oil and egg yolks. The skins were trampled to ensure that the paste penetrated the skin fully. Alum was an expensive ingredient brought by traders from the Mediterranean, most specifically from Greece.

The skins were then slaked or perched. Slaking entailed drawing it over a semi-circular blunt blade set into a wooden block. This helped to soften the hide and make it supple. Perching entailed draping the skin across a frame or 'perch', then scraping with a blade. Tawyers were also permitted to process the skins from 'casualty' animals – animals that had died of natural causes – as well as those skins removed during butchery.

It is interesting to note that tawed leather, the softer leather that was not tanned but preserved with fats and oils, was not subject to this level of scrutiny. Glovers, purse-makers, coffer-makers, stationers and similar artisans were largely unregulated in this way, and as a result there are records to show that the market was flooded with 'counterfeit leather' and poor quality, badly preserved soft leather goods. Despite all the rules surrounding tanning and leatherworking, there were still massive problems. In 1372, the mayor of London instituted penalties for the preparation and sale of sheep and calf leather that had been scraped and dyed to look like roe leather. Tawyers who worked for furriers were made liable to imprisonment if they prepared old furs into leather; they were also not allowed to remove heads from the skins they dressed, so that it was impossible to pass one type of animal skin off as another.

English Medieval Industries: Craftsmen, Techniques, Products

Once processed, the leather was cut and stitched with waxed thread to make a wide variety of items, such as shoes. It was stuck to wooden items such as boxes with animal glue, often made from the very hooves and flesh scrapings that had been the by-products of the tanning trade. Leather was also moulded into different shapes. This entailed soaking the leather to saturation point then, once it became stretchy and elastic, moulding it over forms made from wood, metal or plaster. The leather could be decorated whilst damp by stamping or embossing. It was then allowed to dry slowly and would stay in the shape of the form used. This method was used very effectively to make containers for liquids, such as bottles and buckets, or tankards and other drinking vessels.

Another moulding process used in the period was a method called *cuir bouilli*. It was sometimes used to make items of armour. It has been suggested (Cheshire, 2014) that the *cuir bouilli* method used rawhide which was warmed in water. Translated from the Norman French, *cuir* means 'skin', and *boilli* means 'boiled'. This has sometimes led to confusion, with the translation being 'boiled leather', and of course boiled leather armour would be useless as it would be brittle and unable to combat fired arrows. That has led some commentators to imagine that *cuir bouilli* refers to moulded leather, as detailed above. Cheshire (2014, 80) also suggested that in some parts of the medieval world, notably Palestine, *cuir bouilli* was made with rawhide but then an extra layer made from crushed stone and glue was added for extra protection. This method, tested in the modern era by Cheshire's team, makes a material that resists penetration from fired arrows up to six times more than leather alone. The distinctive lamellar armour worn traditionally by Japanese Samurai was made from scales made from boiled rawhide treated using this method (as well as metals such as iron) which made very strong, protective armour.

Medieval shoemakers were subject to regulations and inspection in the same way as the tanners were. Shoemakers at the time came in three groups: cordwainers, corvesers and cobblers. Cordwainers and corvesors made new shoes from leather and cobblers repaired shoes or made shoes from reclaimed and recycled leather. Cordwainers were the 'designer label' shoe makers of the era, with their name being derived originally from the Spanish workers of Cordovan leather. At the other end of the scale in terms of shoemakers were the cobblers, who were permitted to mend shoes, but not to make them from new leather. In 1409 regulations were introduced in London to stop any overlap of these two types of shoe making, enforcing a division between the two crafts.

Leather could be highly ornamented in the medieval era. It was often coloured with dye; red was particularly popular. It was also sometimes painted with tempera, which was made from pigment mixed with some sort of water-soluble binder such as egg yolk. In bookbinding, it was also often gilded, with either glaire – egg white – or gold size being used to attach gold leaf. Leather was also embossed and stamped, incised, punched and embossed to make patterns and shapes for decorative purposes.

So, in the Medieval era, leather continued to be an important commodity in terms of usage and trade. Regulations were introduced to govern the production and working of leather, but these were not always effective. The use of leather working for book binding in the era increased hugely, and new ways of decorating and finishing leather were introduced, paving the way for the lavish work of the Tudor leather industry to come.

Chapter 3

Tudor and Stuart Leathercraft

Leathercraft was of huge importance in Tudor times, and the industry was widespread, with leather and leather goods being made across the country. Leather workers were found in most villages, but leathercrafting as an industry was largely urban, as it worked alongside the large-scale butchery of animals for food. The main markets for the sale of leather goods were, of course, in the towns. London held huge numbers of tanners and leatherworkers. By the Stuart period, in the seventeenth century, there were 3,000 shoemakers in the city, and the same number of glovemakers and leather dressers. Tanneries were widespread in the city. By the late seventeenth century, there were eighty in Bermondsey and Southwark alone – the stench and the polluted water must have been unbearable.

> 'in most villages of the realm there is some one dresser or worker of leather, and ... in most of the market towns three, four, or five, and many great towns 10 or 20, and in London and the suburbs ... to the number of 200 or very near.'

Lansd. MS., 74, 55.

It was not just London that had many tanneries and leatherworkers. Other cities were in a similar position. Chester was a centre for leather making and leatherworking during this period. Such was the status of leatherworkers in the period that in the hundred years between

1550-1650, a fifth of the people who were given 'freedom of the city' were leatherworkers of one type or another.

The importance of the leather industry in Tudor and Stuart England is corroborated by the creation of a body of legislation controlling the industry. The Leather Act 1563 created a set of rules for the manufacture and sale of leather and leather goods, for example, building upon earlier regulations.

Leathercraft had reach great heights of intricacy and decoration. We are fortunate to have a wealth of information about Tudor leathercraft from a combination of sources, including archaeological finds, documentation and such was the importance of the leather industry that we even have Acts of Parliament from the period concerning the production of leather and leather goods.

Both dressed and tanned leather was widely used during this era. The difference between the two was as follows: tanned leather was created via the process of crushing bark in water and steeping the hide. Dressed leather was the preparation of skins with oil, egg yolk, alum and other materials. Heavy leathercraft (such as saddlery and harness) used tanned leather, and light leathercraft (such as the production of fine gloves) could use soft dressed leather. It is interesting to note that during the Tudor period, the concentration of tanneries in iron smelting areas was high. This may well be connected to the use of oak trees in both industries. Where the oak was used for creating charcoal to smelt iron, oak bark was plentiful so it could be ground to make soaks for tanneries.

We have a great deal of evidence about life in Tudor times, including leather goods, from the wreck of *The Mary Rose*. She was a Tudor warship built in 1510 which sailed in the service of King Henry VIII of England for thirty-four years before sinking in 1545. It was discovered again by the modern world in 1971 and was finally raised in 1982. This stunning monument to the Tudor Age stands now in the museum built to house it on Portsmouth's historic dockyard. The ship contained a wealth of military and everyday objects that had lain hidden beneath the waves for 437 years, resting under a blanket of silt that helped to preserve the treasure she held for modern eyes. Excavation work carried out between 1979 and 1982 equated to an amazing twelve 'person years' on the seabed, making a stunning 28,000 dives.

Among finds from the ship were many vegetable-tanned leather items, which was the primary method of tanning, particularly for high end quality leather goods in the period. Although some dressed leather was used, it would not have lasted for long once immersed in the salt water. Finds from the wreck included a huge range of items: a leather drum case, straps, pouches, knife sheaths and scabbards, wine flasks, bottles, buckets, highly tooled and decorated calfskin book covers, archers' bracers, straps, falconry mittens, and four hundred and twenty-five shoes and boots, including nine well-preserved leather thigh boots. Interestingly, a quantity of leather discs punched with holes were found. At first, archaeologists did not know what these were, but then one of the discs was found with arrows, both whole and broken, threaded through the holes. The archaeologists realised that these cleverly designed and functional discs were used to separate the arrows inside a quiver, so that they could be withdrawn and used quickly in battle, without damaging any of the flights. The incredible variety of finds from *The Mary Rose* gives us a window into the leatherwork of the era, from the intricately crafted to functional, every day pieces.

Northampton has traditionally been an area where shoe making has made up a large part of industry. This was true from as early as the Tudor era. Records show that shoemaking was the leading industrial occupation in the town in 1524 with hides, skins and oak bark all readily available locally. Notably, in 1642, thirteen shoemakers from the town were given a contract to make 600 pairs of boots and 4,000 pairs of shoes for the army going to Ireland for the Civil War. However, the ubiquitous tanneries and leather dressers in the town created problems in terms of public health. Local authorities regularly attacked the industry for polluting water supplies with their processes and leaving animal carcasses lying in public places.

Sussex was also a busy place in Tudor times for the creation of leather and leather goods, perhaps due once again to the rural nature of the area. Hides were plentiful and Sussex oak bark was particularly high in tannins and therefore perfect for the treatment of leather. A great deal of leather and leather goods made in Sussex were exported directly from the ports of Sussex such as Rye, and records of the Privy Council at the time dealt regularly with the smuggling of leather to avoid taxes and duties. In 1697, an incredible 154 petitions were sent to Parliament from towns and villages across the country protesting against the levying of excise duty.

So, what did Tudors use leather for? The upper classes wore fashionable jerkins made from leather. These tight-fitting waistcoats were made from the softest leather, and were worn over doublets – fitted, highly decorated and often embroidered jackets. They had no sleeves, and were often slashed or had holes punched in them to show the decorative clothing beneath. Collars were decorative, and worn high on the neck. Working men also wore a type of loose leather jerkin, but this was worn over a tunic rather than a doublet. These 'buff-jerkins' protected them as they worked. Leather was also used to shape the figures of wealthy ladies of the period. These women wore uncomfortable *basquine* under their clothes – leather and whalebone corsets to accentuate tiny waists under broader shoulders.

Glove making employed many of the poorest people in the country, with whole families being involved in the manufacture of gloves from leather and kid. Hereford and Oxfordshire were particularly rich in glove makers. These rural areas were home to many small farmers, looking for ways to supplement their income. Readily available calfskin made this easier. Harness and saddles were also developing quickly in the Tudor and Stuart era, and becoming more sophisticated. The modern western saddle developed from Spanish saddles taken to the Americas originally by Conquistadores, for example.

Archaeologists from the Museum of London have excavated a treasure trove of items from a site near Tower Bridge, including beautifully preserved Tudor era leather items. The dig was a two-acre site that had been a fish farm, called Pike Garden, serving the culinary needs of the affluent. When the property was sold in 1560, the fish tanks were used as rubbish tips. Rubbish was also dumped into a nearby sewer when it closed in 1610. When ground was broken for a new hotel complex on the site in 2009, archaeologists began to dig and found thousands of objects dating from the 1480s to the early 1600s. Many items were well preserved, due to the waterlogged site. More than 400 leather shoes were discovered, many looking like modern footwear. Leather and suede shoes with buckles and laces were found, as well as some with curiously curled points still stuffed with moss. Early Tudor shoes did not have heels and were mostly quite flat, but by the late sixteenth century many shoes had higher heels. During the excavation, saddle parts, leather fringes and fragments were also found, helping to build a detailed picture of Tudor leatherwork used by all strata of society.

During Elizabeth I's reign, the leather industry was once more embroiled in controversy, counterfeiting and shady dealing. The Leathersellers' Company had become dominated by a few wealthy and well-connected members who engineered and grasped a monopoly of the leather trade for themselves. They forced up leather prices by buying the majority of tanned leather being produced. The tawed skin trade was in an equally crooked state. The Leathersellers' Company had also gained a monopoly in this industry, and forced leatherworkers such as glovers to buy their dressed skins in bundles of a dozen, which often included *linings*, or poor quality, unusable skins.

They even took part in the actual counterfeiting of leather. They allowed dog skin, fish skin, calf skin and others to be dressed to look like expensive Spanish Seville skins, worth double, by having the skins dressed:

> 'with the powder of date stones and of gaule and with French shomake that is nothinge like the Spannish shomake, to give them a pretie sweete savor but nothinge like to the civile skynnes, and the powder of theise is of veary smale price and the powder of right Spannish shomake grounded in a mill is wourth the weight, which shomake is a kynd of brush, shrubb, or heath in Spayne and groweth low by the ground and is swete like Gale [myrtle] in Cambridgshire and is cutt twise a yeare and soe dried and grounded into powder by milles and dresseth all the Civile and Spannish skynnes brought hither.'

Lansd. MS.

This led to a great outcry, and demands for the tawed hide industry to be governed in the same way as the tanned leather industry.

During the Tudor and Stuart periods, the world was being explored and 'discovered' – no doubt news to the people that already lived there – at an amazing rate. In 1492 North America was 'discovered' for King Ferdinand and Queen Isabella of Spain by Christopher Columbus. The native American people who lived there had first colonised the continent by crossed the Bering Strait from Asia in prehistoric times. America had also been previously visited before this 'discovery' by Viking Erik the Red in the tenth century and Basque whalers who first saw Maine in the fourteenth century, yet it is Columbus who is credited with its discovery.

European sailors and fishermen had been trading for furs with tribes off the coast of north-eastern Canada since the 1500s. The fishermen traded metal cooking utensils, guns and cloth for beaver, fox, ermine and sable. The trade became so successful that many of the fishermen became full time fur traders.

Henry VIII may have established England as a mighty sea power, becoming a thorn in the side of Spain's armada, but it was his daughter Elizabeth who used exploration to drive into the New World. In 1585, Elizabeth knighted her favourite, Sir Walter Raleigh. Raleigh acted as her instrument in the English colonisation of North America, being granted a royal patent to explore the territory he rather sycophantically named *Virginia*, after his queen. This paved the way for future English settlements.

Raleigh commissioned Richard Hakluyt, an Elizabethan historian to write his 'Discourse on Western Planting', an account that described the Americas in glowing terms, as a source of great riches. The treatise also attacked the Spanish policies there with regard to the native Americans and stated that Elizabeth should give 'every assistance' to them.

The first attempt to establish a colony at Roanoke was a failure, and by 1590 it had failed completely. No successful colonisation happened during Elizabeth's reign, but King James I would continue with the attempt and send colonists to settle the Americas – and this time they were successful, with the colony of Virginia being established in 1607, four years after her death.

The native American people that the explorers and subsequent settlers encountered were skilled leathercrafters. They worked with butter-soft, honey coloured buckskin, the likes of which had never been seen by the settlers. A settler at the time wrote about the native Americans in his journal:

> 'They goe all naked save their privityes, yet in coole weather they weare deare skinns, with the hayre on loose: some have leather stockinges vp to their twistes, & sandalls on their feet.'

In 1664, the English conquered 'New Netherland' and renamed it New York. The English traded with the Iroquois in northern New York, and Algonkian-speaking tribes in New England.

The northern tribes, such as the Cheyenne people, were skilled in their curing of skins and hides, particularly buckskin and furs from smaller animals such as rabbits and squirrels. The animals used depended on the animals hunted in a particular locale. Cherokee and Iroquois people used deerskin; people who lived on the plains used buffalo skin, and Inuits in the far north of Alaska used seal and caribou skin. The skins from moose, elk, antelope, caribou and bighorn sheepskin were also used. Some tribes also used large skins such as elk, caribou or buffalo to cover the frames of their tipis.

Hides were preserved with brains from the hunted animals, plant material and wood smoke. Furs were also treated with smoke and rubbed with brains, but were treated differently to ensure that the hair did not fall out of the skins.

The actual garments made and worn also depended on the local climate. In some areas, men wore breechcloths only; in cooler areas they wore trousers and tunics. Women might wear skirts, trousers or tunics. Both sexes wore moccasin shoes, sewn together with sinew and sometimes soled with rawhide for durability. In colder areas, mukluks, boots made from sealskin, reindeer hide and fur, were worn. Leather clothing was often decorated with fringes cut into the leather, with added wood, shell and stone beads. Native American bags were often made from leather; either tanned bags made from mainly deer or elk skin or stiffer containers made from parfleche, a type of rawhide. Bags were often decorated with beading, painted or quilled.

Tanning was carried out in a variety of ways, and different tribes developed different tools and methods, yet there was some commonality. Hides were scraped free of flesh and fat whilst stretched on a frame, on a beam or tree. Bone or wooden tools were used to scrape away the flesh, and in some cases the hides were then soaked in a solution of ash and water to help remove hairs and open the pores of the skin. Some tribes smoked skins. This is still practised today on moose skins in Canada.

The Comanche tribe were known to use burnt lime rocks in their process, and the Klallam people soaked their hides in a solution of boiled fern leaves. Some tribes soaked hides in a boiled sweetcorn solution, which went sour. This soak was similar to the soured grains or beer soak used in Europe at the same time. Whether acid or alkali was used, the soak's purpose was to break down the glue-type surface of the buckskin and make it easier to work with the brains rub that came next in the process.

Brains were made into a solution with water, and rubbed into the hides. Most tribes used this method, adding different ingredients to the solution. Spinal fluid, bone marrow, tallow, fats, oil and crushed acorns were used by different groups, according to availability. People from the Gulf of Georgia used sea mammal and fish oils. Tonto Apache people used berries and tribes south of the Colorado River used saguaro cactus seeds. Some tribes used decayed fir wood, and others used wild rhubarb. As in all locations around the globe, people adapted the materials available locally and used them to meet their needs.

After soaking with brains, the skins were softened. Tools were used to rub and scrape the hides to make it supple and pliable. Once again, materials were chosen according to availability. Pumice stone, mussel shells, flint shard and flakes, slate, knapped stone, bone, antler, sandstone and turtle shells have all been identified as hide softening tools. Hides were also stretched on pole frames at this point.

Bark dyes were used to colour hides in many cases, but it is unclear as to whether this resulted in a full 'tan' – but any soak in tannin-laded water would have changed the constituency and qualities of the hide. Many plants were used to create different shades: aptly named leather root; mistletoe, white maple, alder, paper birch, ferns, sumach, hemlock, indigo bush, mahogany, elm, elder, ironwood, oak, willow, ephedra, lemonade berry, canaigre, honey mesquite and Oregon grape.

Buckskin items were also painted decoratively. Plant materials and ground rocks were used to create a wide range of pigment. Red ochre was crushed, creating a dark red from ground minerals; clays would also be used. Walnuts created a deep black and bloodroot created a red. (Diemer-Eaton, 2010)

By 1763, the British had claimed Canada and the Midwest from the French, and British traders entered the Great Lakes fur trade, shipping the beautiful furs used for clothing the wealthy back to Britain. The United States claimed dominion over the region after the American Revolution in 1783, but in 1794, they signed Jay's Treaty with Great Britain which allowed British traders to continue to work in the Midwest. British companies would control the fur trade there until 1815. By the 1850s the fur trade was over. The native Americans now lived on reservations and were no longer able to hunt and harvest furs on their old, largely over-hunted territories.

Leather working was still an important industry in the Tudor era; by Elizabethan times it was an important part of trade, with many hides being brought from the *New World*. In recent times we have learned a great deal about leather working techniques used by Native American tribes, still used by traditional leather workers in the US today.

Leather grew increasingly ornamented and complex in Tudor and Stuart times, and we are fortunate to have many well-preserved leather items from the period in collections around the world. Maritime archaeology has greatly expanded our knowledge of tools and working from the period, especially due to amazing sea bed excavations and the raising of *The Mary Rose*.

Chapter 4

Georgian Era Leathercraft

In the Georgian era, the manufacture of leather and leather goods was the most lucrative English industry, after textiles. It was also one of the largest employers of labour, second only to agricultural labour. In 1974, Clarkson's study *The English Bark Trade 1680-1830* drew together information about bark sales and purchases from tannery accounts and estate records and upon records of excise duties. In England, Wales and Ireland, the demand for bark in the 1720s and 30s fluctuated between 55,000 and 60,000 tons per annum, at a value of between £165,000 and £198,000. By the early 1790s, this had risen to 80,000 tons, with a value of around £300,000. Oak bark was available as a by-product of the timber and fuel industry. A 40-year-old tree would yield around 9lb to 12lb of bark per cubic foot. Trees were marked for peeling and this work was sometimes done by 'peelers' whilst the trees were still standing as it was easier, but they were also felled and then peeled. Peelers used an iron tool called a 'spud' which was a 2ft-long rod with a heart-shaped head. It prised off lengths of bark that were about 2ft long, which were then dried and broken up into pieces in a process called 'hatching'. The 2-3in pieces were then stored in bags ready to be sold. In the latter half of the eighteenth century, most bark was milled instead of hatched. Some mills had grindstones that were horse powered; others were powered by water.

Rusland Tannery in the Lake District tanned 'heavy leather' from cow and horse hides in the Georgian period, and it had a nearby supply of oak bark from the land in the southern area of the lakes, which was coppiced commercially. There were also readily available hides from local slaughterhouses and a good water supply.

Flayed hides were washed in a nearby stream, which was a heavy task, as even dry hides could weigh up to 50lbs. The hides were then suspended by chains from iron bars and dipped into lime pits. There are the remains of two pits at Rusland, just south of the stream. The tannery had an unusual Penrith sandstone surface used for de-hairing and fleshing. A two-handled blade was used to scrape off flesh fragments, which were sent to be used as glue or gelatin, and the hair was removed with a blunt blade and sent to be used to make mortar or for upholstery. A scudder then used a curved slate blade to remove lime and waste from the heavy hides. The hides were then trimmed into usable parts, or 'rounded,' and then tanned. At Rusland there were eight slate and timber lined pits for tanning, with a narrowed cobbled path between, with a drain. After tanning, they would be washed and scoured, then dried. Rusland had a drying room with louvred doors. After drying, skins would be rolled and oiled.

The Georgian era is seen by historians as a period of massive expansion in manufacturing, when shopping became almost a hobby for those who could afford it. A prosperous middle class was emerging and they had money to spare for leisure pursuits – and shopping was a favourite social activity in the markets and shops that began to proliferate in the era. Gorgeous, glass-fronted shops displayed their wares and hanging signs and trade advertisements became popular. Shopping – especially extravagant shopping – became a way to display wealth and social status. Specialist shops catered for their niche trade. Rapid expansion in the manufacture of consumer goods meant that the age of mass consumption had arrived – and so had the dedicated shoe shop.

Shoes were extravagant in the Georgian era, with men and women alike wearing heels. Many of these were made of highly decorated leather. At the lesser end of the market, shoemakers produced 'off the peg' shoes and boots, ready for walk-in purchases. Made to measure shoes were also available, made on wooden lasts made to the size of the customer's feet. The lasts could be changed over time, if the customer's foot size or shape changed. Pieces of leather padding could be added and pieces of wood removed or shaved away.

High heels were popular from 1720 onwards. The 'Louis' heel was a popular style, which was a concave shaped heel. It took its name from Louis XIV, as they were first designed for him. Some heels were very tall indeed, and they were popular with men and women at the French court, including Louis XV's mistress, Madame de Pompadour. That of course made them popular with fashionable folk throughout Europe. They were made from painted leather, silks and damask and had extravagant buckles and bows.

In the early 1800s, flat, low heeled 'ballet'-type slippers decorated with a bow or flower were popular for young ladies for indoor wear. They were dainty and made from soft kid or silk, and wore out easily. Outdoors, half boots were *de rigeur*. As the Regency era began in 1810, flat soled boots often made from brightly coloured leather were worn by fashionable women. Boots were so popular that even bridal boots and dancing boots were made. They often also had matching reticules, small elegant bags were another popular fashion item of the time, with many made from soft leather.

The most famous boots in the world were made during the Georgian era: the Wellington boot. They were made for the Duke of Wellington and were a modification of the boots worn by Hessian soldiers, designed by the duke himself. The first boots were made from soft calf skin, and they fitted the leg closely. The fashion spread like wildfire and every British gentleman wanted a pair. The name 'Wellingtons' or 'wellies' is still with us, but now describes long waterproof boots made from rubber, latex and neoprene.

Another popular fashion accessory of the time was long, elbow length leather gloves for women. Again, the fashion began in France; this time with the Empress Josephine. At Napoleon and Josephine's coronation in 1804, the gloves cost thirty-three francs per pair, which was rather costly. Napoleon himself owned 240 pairs of gloves. The fashion soon spread across the fashionable salons of Europe. Kidskin was the material of choice in Jane Austen's England, but cloth gloves were also popular. The gloves were often made to fit loosely around the arm so they could be scrunched up fashionably towards the wrist. Both men and women wore gloves, and it deemed 'poor breeding' to go out without wearing them.

The glove industry in Britain was centred around Worcester, where nearly half of all British glove makers were based. Between 1790 and 1820, there were 150 manufacturers, employing over 30,000 people in and around Worcester. Overseas trade in gloves was controlled with large taxes to protect the British glovemakers from competition and Worcester prospered. The tax was lifted in 1826 and the reduction in trade resulted in mass unemployment in Worcester.

The Mary Rose, from the Tudor era, was not the only 'museum beneath the waves' as far as leather is concerned. During the Georgian era, The *Metta Catharina*, a two-masted brigantine sank in Plymouth Sound in 1786, under Raven's Cliffs on the Cornish side. It had been built in Scandinavia in 1782. A story appeared in the newspaper *The Sherbourne Mercury*, then the ship was forgotten. In 1973 divers from the British Sub Aqua Club were searching for the wreck of the HMS *Harwich* which had sunk in 1691. They found a ship's bell and when it was cleaned the wreck they discovered was provisionally identified as the *Catarina von Flensburg*.

The ship's cargo was a haul of neatly wrapped hides that had been preserved in the dark silt for 200 years. Some of the tanned hides were as large as cattle and complete with heads and tails – and bore the initials of the tanners who prepared them. Research has revealed that the skins are reindeer leather, preserved and tanned in the traditional Russian method using willow bark and birch oil. The leather is supple and the colour varies from light sienna to claret. Many of the hides are cross hatched, consistent with the grain seen on book bindings and upholstery from the period. This effect was produced by using wooden rollers during the leather making process. Russian leather was famed for its ability to resist water and insects, as they dislike the smell of the birch oil used to curry it.

The wreck was determined to belong to Prince Charles, as Duke of Cornwall. He waived rights to the leather so it could be studied further. Archaeologists involved with the project sold some of the hides to specially selected traditional leatherworkers, which not only helped to finance further excavation of the site, but also allowed the leather to be explored by the crafters to find out about the quality and properties of the material. Robin Snelson, a local leatherworker examined the leather. He washed it in fresh water to remove the salt from the ocean, and dressed it with lanolin.

At the time when the ship sank, Russia was a leading exporter of fur, timber, tar, hemp and leather. Once St Petersburg was built, export from the port was brisk. Russian leather was highly prized. The process of making the leather in this way was sadly lost during the Russian Revolution. With support from the Heritage Lottery Fund, some of the leather is displayed at Edgcumbe House, near to where the ship sank.

Chapter 5

Victorian Era Leathercraft

In the Victorian era, tanning and leatherwork in Britain underwent great changes, becoming hugely industrialised. Small, local artisan run tanneries and leatherworking were replaced by centralised factories that came to dominate whole areas of cities around the country. The coming of the railways allowed the leather trade – and many others of course – to grow exponentially. Raw materials and finished goods could be shipped around the country, and the world, as the result of the growth of the integrated transport system.

In big cities such as London, whole swathes of the city by the Victorian era had become grim, stinking industrial hovels. By the mid nineteenth century, Bermondsey, down by the Thames, had become a slum area filled with the stink of local factories. Shipbuilding, engineering, food processing and rope making took place here, but the worst of these industries in terms of pollution were the tanneries. Bermondsey had developed originally due to the establishment of tanneries in the fifteenth century and had become London's main area for leatherworking. By the 1790s, Bermondsey was responsible for a third of the country's leather production and became known as 'The Land of Leather'. Even the local church, St Crispin's, was dedicated to the patron saint of leather and shoes. By the Victorian era there was an explosion in production in the leatherworking industry, with the need for leather parts for machines in factories. Bermondsey now housed Europe's largest leather industry.

It was a perfect place for tanning and leatherworking, as it was on the river, so there was an endless supply of the water which was needed for the tanning process. In the beginning, rural Bermondsey had herds of cattle and many oak trees for bark. There was more space than in the city and this meant there was room for the industry to expand.

By the Victorian era, cheap labour could be found nearby, as the area was very poor and people lived in filthy slum housing. Coal porters, labourers, sailors and costermongers lived in Bermondsey as well as the factory workers.

People slept four and five to a room, and sometimes more, in cramped, insanitary conditions. There could be as few as one water standpipe for twenty-five houses, which were completely without sanitation. Combine those conditions with the stench of the tanneries and factories, and it must have been like living in hell itself. In 1832 a Reform Bill had made Bermondsey a part of the borough of Southwark. The population of the borough swelled from 27,465 in 1851 to 136,660 by 1891. Tenement blocks were raised to house the workers, but these were dark, unsanitary places where disease and poverty were rife. Charles Dickens's *Oliver Twist* immortalised Jacob's Island, a slum area of Bermondsey. Conditions in the factories themselves were often poor; they were badly ventilated, stinking, crowded and dirty. Dickens described Bermondsey Leather Market itself in his Dictionary of London, 1879:

'This great leather, or rather hide market, lies in Weston-street, ten minutes' walk from the Surrey side of London-bridge. The neighbourhood in which it stands is devoted entirely to thinners and tanners, and the air reeks with evil smells. The population is peculiar, and it is a sight at twelve o'clock to see the men pouring out from all the works. Their clothes are marked with many stains; their trousers are discoloured by tan; some have apron and gaiters of raw hide; and about them all seems to hang a scent of blood. The market itself stands in the centre of a quiet block of buildings on the left-hand side of Weston-street, the entry being through a gateway. Through this a hundred yards down, a square is reached. Most of it is roofed, but there is an open space lathe centre. Under the roofing are huge piles of fresh hides and sheep-skins. There is no noise or bustle, and but few people about. There are no retail purchasers, the sales being almost entirely made to the great tanners in the neighbourhood. The warehouses round are all full of tanned hides; the yards behind the high walls are all tanneries, with their tens of thousands of hides soaking in the pits. Any visitor going down to look at the Bermondsey hide-market should, if possible, procure beforehand an order to visit one of the great tanning establishments. Unless this be done the visit to the market itself will hardly repay the trouble of the journey, or make up for the unpleasantness of the compound of horrible smells which pervade the whole neighbourhood.'

Dickens's Dictionary of London, 1879

Animals were slaughtered, flayed and their skins processed in the area around Weston Street, at the Leather Market, close to London Bridge. The smell of blood, faeces, ash, lime and urine filled the air. Henry Mayhew, the great chronicler of the lives of those living in poverty in London walked the streets of Bermondsey in the 1850s. He was struck by the foul atmosphere around the tanneries:

'On every side are seen announcements of the carrying on of the leather trade; the peculiar smell of raw hides and skins, and of tan pits, pervades the atmosphere, and the monotonous click of the steam engines used in grinding bark assails the ear.'

There were many tanneries in Bermondsey in the Victorian leather manufacturing boom-era. Tens of thousands of skins were soaked in great pits as part of the tanning that took place there. John and Thomas Hepburn had a tannery, established in the eighteenth century, on Long Lane, where it stood along with an astonishing ten other tanneries. From 1865 James Garnar ran a tannery at The Grange. In 1806 the Bevington Brothers began a tanning operation at Neckinger Mills which was a former paper mill. The water from the Neckinger tidal stream had powered the papermill and was now used to create leather. The Bevingtons drove innovation at their factory, patenting a machine of their own to split hides, furs and leather during production. The operation moved only out of Bermondsey to Leicester in the 1970s.

Trades related to the leather from the tanneries also flourished in Bermondsey. Fellmongers, parchment makers, curriers, hat makers (using the by-products of hair and wool) were all established in the area. By-products such as horns were used to make combs, spoons, handles and musical instruments. Hooves were used to make glue – so little of the animal remains was wasted. There was even work for 'pure collectors' – a euphemistic name for the poorest in society who collected dog faeces to sell to tanners for use in the leather making process. Pigeon droppings were also bought by tanneries for processing skins. An advertisement in *The Scotsman* newspaper in 1872 was offering £4 per ton!

The waste was used for *bating* and *puering* the skins. After the hides were scraped clean of flesh and fat, and soaked in lime pits to relax and open the pores ready to de-hair them, they were soaked in solutions containing droppings. This also de-limed the skins. The largest skins, such as cow hides, were bated by soaking them in cold water and pigeon dung for around ten days. Smaller skins were soaked in a solution of warm water and dog faeces in a process called *puering* – no doubt, where the strange name of 'pure' collectors came from, in a job that would be anything but!

The *bater* or *puerer* was a skilled worker who had to judge the concentration of the solutions carefully – too concentrated and the skins would be damaged; too weak, and the process would not be effective. It is incredible to think that this process only died out as a common practice in factories when pancreol bates were introduced in the 1920s. Thinking about the ingredients used in the tanning process might make that Victorian leather case seem a little less elegant, perhaps.

After this process was completed, the hides would be scudded. This means they were worked over a beam with a semi-circular knife, or later, worked by a scudding machine. The descriptively and somewhat repulsively named 'scud' which was removed was made up of fats, salts, lime, gelatine and hair follicles.

After scudding the hides were beaten to soften them and then they would go into the tanning pits. The skins would be lifted into pits filled with a solution of oak bark and water and would be moved from time to time by men with tongs. It was back-breaking work, as the saturated hides were very heavy. The movement helped to make sure that the hides were soaked evenly. The hides were steeped in a weak solution first, for between four and six months and then they were removed and put into a stronger solution. Then the hides would be layered with oak bark and stacked in deep pits filled with a strong tanning solution. These remained in place for around four months for a light hide, with longer for heavier skins. Ox-hides were thick and heavy and could take a year and the heaviest hides could take up to two years. Tanneries generally had their own bark mills where the bark was processed by grinding it into a powder. This dust was dangerous and unpleasant if it was inhaled and it was highly flammable.

The tanning pits were around 6ft deep. Before machinery was introduced, pumpers and water bearers would empty and fill the pits. Steam power made these workers redundant, as the tanks were fitted with waste pipes and hose supplies to fill and empty the liquid.

An article in *The Scotsman* newspaper, written in the 1860s, describes innovations in tanning being developed at the time in Gorgie Mills, near Edinburgh. The proprietors, J. and G. Cox were experimenting with machinery to mechanise the arduous and costly tanning process. They developed a system for attaching hides to a drum and suspending them thus in a tanning solution. The skins were also pressed on the drum. The article credits the same gentlemen with the innovation of creating tanning bags – however, this was a re-introduction of an old lost technique rather than an invention, strictly speaking, as this was an ancient practice. After the puering process had taken place, small skins were sewn into bag-like shapes and any holes sewn shut. The skins were then filled with tanning liquor via a leg hole and were sealed. The idea was that the pressure would force the tanning solution into the pores of the skin. The skin 'bottles' were dropped into a weak tanning solution for a day and stirred with wooden poles. They were lifted out at night and left to drain. The bags were released and filled daily for three to four days to aid the tanning process. At the end of the period they were cut open and drained, leaving behind leather that had been tanned using a quick, if labour-intense process. Another innovator, listed in the article as Mr Boak, was credited as the inventor of a wheel that kept hides moving in a tanning trough to soak it more efficiently in the tanning liquor.

After tanning, the skins were shaved to obtain a uniform thickness in the hides. The shaving was carried out over a flat beam with a special 'T'-shaped knife, and the shavers measured the thickness by its feel. Larger tanneries introduced splitting machines that cut thick hide into layers in the 1860s, and shaving machines in the 1890s. The machines were not as accurate as hand shaving and still needed skilled operatives to finish the work.

After the skins were tanned and shaved, they would be *curried* to finish the surface. Until the 1820s, the currying had to be carried out in separate premises, due to the separation by law of tanning and currying. Currying was still done by hand. When the hides arrived, they would be weighed, graded and examined, and selected for a purpose such as making harness leather, shoe leather etc. According to its purpose, the hide would be trimmed or *rounded*. Hides being dressed for harness, for example, would have the softer, stretchier belly parts trimmed away as they would not be strong enough, even after processing, for harness leather, which needed to be robust and durable.

After the skins had been shaved and soaked, they were scoured. This smoothed and flattened the skins. Warm water, smooth stones, glass pebbles, wooden slickers and brushes were used to stretch out the skins to make a flat smooth surface. Both the grain and flesh sides were smoothed in this way. By the 1860s, scouring machines were beginning to be introduced in tanneries. Again, these early machines could not achieve the same fine results as hand scoured leather.

After scouring, the hides were soaked again, but this time for a couple of days, in a weak tanning solution to brighten the grain and replace tans lost by scouring. Then the skins would be rubbed with dubbin, a mixture of tannin and fish oil. This was brushed onto the hides which were then hung in sheds to dry. As the water evaporated, the oils would sink further into the grain of the hide. Once dried, it would be rubbed again with a slicker to remove excess fats. Currying was heavy, labour intensive work, but it was skilled and well paid.

Leather was also dyed using vegetable dyes. Logwood from the Caribbean dyed leather a spectrum of yellow through to red depending on the strength of the solution used. Brazilwood gave a reddish-brown hue; indigo offered shades of blue and cochineal beetles gave a carmine red.

Shades could be played with by adding mordants to the process, such as metal salts – iron, aluminium, tin and copper. Leather was dyed in great trays. In the 1850s, leather dyeing was revolutionised by the introduction of synthetic dyes, such as mauveine, processed using coal tar.

Fine leather was also sometimes decorated by being taken to a 'japanning' shop, where it was put through a process called 'japanning'. It was stretched out and nailed onto a board and enamelling was applied. Sometimes as many as eight coats would be added, with each coat needing to be dried before the next was applied. The piece would then be dried in great ovens. 'Japanning' created a shiny black patent leather surface.

The Victorian leather market buildings can still be seen in Bermondsey today. Hepburn and Gale's tannery finally closed its doors in 2007, and aptly named Leathermarket Street is still home to the Leather, Hide and Wool Exchange, built in 1879. This has now converted into accommodation and work space.

Leather was needed for a great many products in the Victorian era. Henry Mayhew, writing in 1850, identified boot and shoe makers as the largest class of artisans, or as he called them 'handicraftsmen', working in Britain at the time. There were 214,780, with 28,574 working in London alone.

Victorian shoemakers used many tools that would be recognised – and used by – leatherworkers today. They used marking wheels, stretching pliers, awls, burnishers and knives to create shoes and boots. Interestingly, as late as 1850, there were no special measures taken to create right and left shoes. All shoes were made on a straight last, which would make the 'breaking in' of new shoes incredibly uncomfortable! The foot itself would have to mould the leather into shape, no doubt warping the foot in the process. Shoes were, however made in two widths. Shoe makers made 'slim' shoes straight onto the last; wider shoes were made by adding a pad to the last before the shoe was made.

Strictly speaking, shoe makers in the Victorian era were still known as *cordwainers*, a term that had existed since the 1100s. A cordwainer, historically, was a person that made new shoes, as distinct from a cobbler, who repaired shoes and used second hand leather. Under the historic guild system, the two professions were separate, and cobblers were forbidden to use new leather and hides. In turn, cordwainers were forbidden to repair shoes.

Artisan shoemakers who made whole shoes from start to finish would often collect materials from the 'manufacturer' and create the shoes in a home workshop. Wives and children would assist in the production of the shoes which, when complete, would be taken back to the manufacturer for payment. These shoe makers could decide their own hours, and work largely autonomously. They were literate, and kept their own records for business purposes, many of which still exist as documents today. Many were granted freemen status and were esteemed members of society.

From the 1850s onwards, mechanisation transformed the craft of shoe making. This threatened the livelihood of artisanal shoe makers. Steam-powered machines could do the stitching previously done by hand, making mass production possible. These independent businessmen protested widely at the idea of working in factories and being controlled by centralised rules and regulations.

In Northampton, a shoe making centre, the protests were vociferous. In 1857, the first shoemaking machines were installed in a large factory by Mr M.P. Mansfield. The local newspaper, the *Northampton Mercury*, carried a report of a meeting held by angry shoemakers. They voiced their fears about mechanisation and how it would affect their livelihoods, but the factory owner was unmoved. In spring 1858, The Northampton Boot and Shoe Makers Mutual Protection Society was formed, to protect the rights of the artisans and to oppose widespread mechanisation. The group made links with shoemakers in other areas, such as Stafford, where a similar battle was taking place. The society instituted a strike fund, preparing for the fight to come.

In early spring 1859, manufacturers announced plans to introduce more machines – this time, machines that would close shoe uppers – formerly, a skilled task. They claimed that without mechanisation, the Northampton shoe industry would fall behind other areas in the country which had already begun to rely on machinery. The society responded by calling strike action, but was unsuccessful. Shoemakers did not answer the call, feeling that their jobs were not threatened. They were wrong.

In 1859, Isaac, Campbell and Company opened a factory in the town. It required all shoemakers that were employed by them to work inside the factory instead of in their own homes. This would enable them to work more efficiently, the factory owners argued, as well as make use of the machines. The company tried to entice workers by reassuring them that women would have separate workshops, with female supervisors, and that married women would still be able to work from home to fulfil their domestic obligations. They insisted that they did not want to enforce a 'factory system', but just wanted to streamline production. There were to be fixed hours and wages, however, thus destroying the autonomy the shoe makers previously enjoyed. Whilst the company closed, another owner, Turner Brothers, stepped in, in 1861. By 1864 there would be an incredible 1,500 closing machines in Northampton, decimating the work previously carried out by artisan cordwainers. By 1865 the Turner Brothers' factory was producing a staggering 100,000 pairs of shoes every week. Although there were still home workers making shoes by hand, mechanisation had won and the factories now ruled the industry.

In the mid-1850s Thomas Crick introduced machines in the shoe making industry in Leicester that would revolutionise production. He used steam-powered rolling machines for hardening leather and cutting machines. In 1853 he introduced a riveting machine, that joined the sole

A collection of images showing the insides of an early twentieth century leather factory.

(*Right*) Etching of a tanner.

(*Below*) A pair of child's slippers from Thebes, *c*.1 AD.

Victorian leather polishing and pebbling machines.

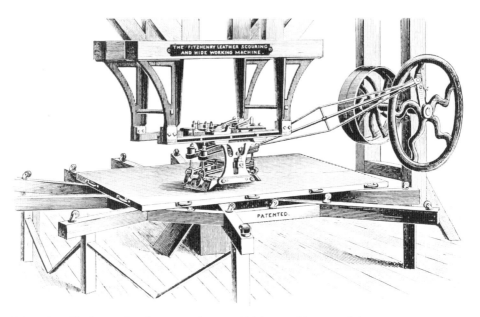

Victorian Fitzhenry leather scouring and hide working machine.

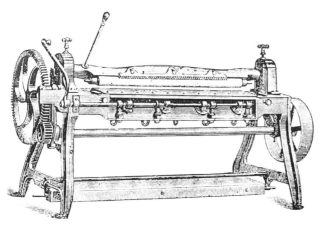

Victorian splitting machine.

Georgian cobblers.

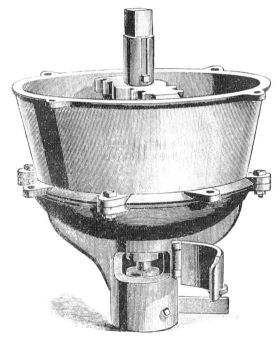

Bark mill for grinding bark to tan leather.

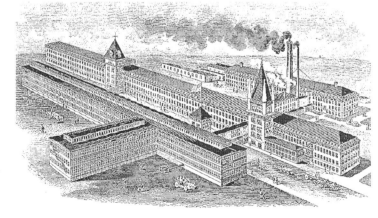

Large-scale production of leather in the Whitman factory, 1911.

Early twentieth century – hides being delivered to the tannery from Chicago, *Shoe and Leather Weekly*, 1912.

(*Above*) Leather finishing room – from the *Popular Science Monthly* magazine, 1892.

(*Below*) Beam House – from the *Popular Science Monthly* magazine, 1892.

Twentieth century
leather tanning,
Yugoslavia.

Skin being stretched
for drying in a
traditional fashion.

Current era parchment being made, as hair is
removed with a bokknife .

Dye vats for leather in Fez, Northern Morocco.

Artisan Jez Hunt from Ancestor Leathercrafts. (*Courtesy of Phil Punton Photography*)

Mark Hunt from Ancestor Leathercrafts. (*Courtesy of Phil Punton Photography*)

Jez Hunt wearing leather crafted items created by Ancestor Leathercrafts. (*Courtesy of Phil Punton Photography*)

Artisan, Andy Bates.

Leather bag by Ancestor Leathercrafts.

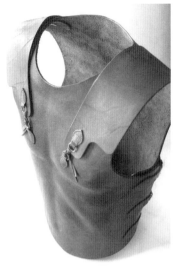

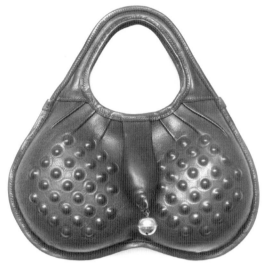

(*Above left*) Leather body armour made by Andy Bates.

(*Above right*) Amazing 'scrotum sack' commission for Grayson Perry by Andy Bates.

(*Above*) An example of leather book binding by Andy Bates.

(*Left*) Intricate helmet and mask by Andy Bates.

Knife sheath by Andy Bates.

to the upper without sewing. This made shoe production even cheaper, but at first retailers were sceptical about the quality of such shoes.

In 1858, the Blake sole sewing machine was invented. This machine attached the inner sole to the outer sole. It was introduced in Leicester by Stead and Simpson, a manufacturer still in business today. This company had begun as curriers and dealers of leather in 1834 and then developed into the shoemaking industry.

In the period 1851 to 1861 the number of people employed in the shoe making industry fell, from 274,000 to 250,000. Whilst this was not the catastrophic fall predicted by those against mechanisation, it was still significant. Many shoes were still being made by workers based at home, despite efforts to gather them together in factories. A class of workers called 'sewers to the trade' were employed from home to sew the uppers of shoes to the soles with waxed thread.

In 1872 Goodyear sewing machines were introduced to England. These were said to be an astonishing fifty-two times faster than hand stitching, using an awl and thread. Goodyear also introduced a chain stitching machine and claimed that these machines could be used to produce boots equal to hand made quality. Production times were falling, but quality was maintained. This was a revolution in terms of profitability and fortunes were made.

In the 1880s, the introduction of factory made shoes brought about more standardization in sizes and widths, so technically shoes became more comfortable. Shoes finally began to be made specifically for the right and left foot. Different types of shoes for different purposes were developed. Sports and sporting activities, such as walking and hiking, became popular and shoes were created specifically for the activity. Boots became a necessity in the active Victorian's wardrobe.

Whilst the wealthy continued to buy handmade shoes, the poorer masses could now buy cheaper shoes made in factories and sold in retail shops where the shoes were not made by the shop keeper. This was a massive change, and whilst it may have made shoes more affordable, it also reduced the piecework labour market for the poor.

Working class families joined 'shoe and boot clubs' where they paid pennies a week and bought shoes regularly, spreading the cost. Shoes would also be handed down as children grew out of them. Shoes often needed repair and there were cobblers to carry out this work. The very poorest people wore second and third hand shoes and clothes, and roughly made items known as 'slops'.

Bridles, saddles and harness were made in huge quantities in the Victorian era, as horses were the primary form of transport. The modern English saddle had begun to be developed in the eighteenth century – first as a response to the rise of fox hunting which required a new type of riding, with hunters needing to be able to jump hedges, ditches, fences and more. Walsall has been the centre of bridle hide and saddlery production for centuries. In Victorian times, horses were the mainstay of transport and the bridle makers of Walsall, mainly based in small workshops and yards did a roaring trade. By 1851, there were seventy-five firms making bridles, saddles and harness, and these goods could be transported around the country – and the world – via the newly built South Staffordshire Railway. By the end of the century, more than 6,000 people were part of the industry, producing equestrian items for the populace as well as in the tens of thousands for the soldiers involved in the Boer Wars.

The leather created was special as the cowhide was treated with a variety of natural greases, tallow (rendered beef or mutton fat) and waxes. It was hard wearing, flexible and water resistant. That made it perfect for saddlery that had to stand up to hard use in all weather conditions. The hides were given to a currier who treated them with a mixture made from oils and fats into the leather over a period of time. This made the leather durable and flexible and able to stand up to the punishment it got once made up into a working saddle.

In the twentieth century, as horses were replaced by cars and vehicles, the bridle industry went into decline. Some producers adapted and turned to making upholstery leather for the automobile industry, but many went out of business. Today, there is also competition from overseas with the importation of large quantities of cheaply produced saddlery from Asia and the Far East, but high end bespoke goods are still made and highly prized around the world.

Chapter 6

Twentieth Century Leathercraft

During the First World War, leather was used for many of the things a soldier would need in the course of his duty – boots, bags and special leather jerkins. These were like body warmers, to help keep the soldier warm and dry. These jerkins, made from leather and lined with khaki wool, helped to insulate against cold and wet.

K.J. Adcock, writing in 1915, in *Leather: From the Raw Material to the Finished Product*, described the way that the tanning and leatherworking industries were still at the time tied in closely to meat production. Adcock described sheep skins as numerous, 'as Great Britain is a big mutton-consuming country', but complained that the number of home-produced hides and skins had been greatly reduced as a result of the increase in import of frozen meat from overseas. The author also bemoaned the British tradition for leaving rind on bacon and pork, as this reduced the quantity of pig skins available for the manufacture of leather!

Adcock complained that the reluctance of the British consumer to cook goat meat meant that this skin was mainly imported for use in the British leather industry, bemoaning the fact that goats could easily be farmed in great numbers in hilly regions of Britain where other less hardy and adaptable animals found it hard to thrive. At the time, goat hides were imported from the Middle and Far east, Austria, Spain and the Cape. It is interesting to note that the author explained that nine-tenths of the 'kid gloves' worn by elegant ladies of the era were in fact made from sheep skin rather than actual kid skin. This did not mean the leather was of a lesser quality; it did however make for a leather that was less durable. Actual goat skin was made into bookbinding material, upholstery, purses, bags, wallets and belts. The writer also described the way in which a great number of skins were exported, despite the needs of British tanners not being met:

> 'Although the domestic supply of hides and skins is quite inadequate to meet the needs of British tanners, a large proportion is exported. American tanners buy large quantities of the best hides and pickled sheep skins. The latter are de-woolled and preserved by a process of pickling with formic or sulphuric acid and salt before exportation. Those preliminary operations are the work of the fellmonger. Nearly all of the horse hides produced in the United Kingdom are, or were before the War, sent to Germany, and British leather-dressers appear to have lost the art of finishing horse hide, or are unable to convert it into leather profitably.'

It is astonishing for the modern reader to read a First World War era account of the conflict between intensive farming methods and other needs, but this is not just a modern concern. Adcock explained that the needs of the farmer – cattle that mature and fatten swiftly – were at odds with the needs of tanners. The cows were fed the unattractively named 'oil cakes', and it was claimed that this led to greasy hides with weaker fibres. This devalued the leather and meant it needed to be soaked in borax before tanning, which reduced the weight of the hides. The same problem was identified in sheep skins, where oily foodstuffs given to the sheep matured them in ten months instead of the standard two years.

Adcock described the variety of 'exotic' leathers imported for use in the leatherworking industry, including such unusual leathers as alligator, walrus and hippopotamus hide. There was a great trade in seal skins from

Newfoundland in America at the time, with an amazing 60,754 skins imported in 1913 according to an American Consular report.

Adcock also discussed vegetable tanning, claiming that oak bark was at this time supplemented with a variety of imported plant materials such as valonia acorn cups from Turkey, to make a stronger tanning solution and therefore a shorter tanning period. Mineral tanning was carried out with chrome salts, formaldehyde, salt, iron and alum, as well as the newly introduced titanium, cerium and potassium salts. In addition to these, an artificial tannin created by combining a sulphonated phenol with formaldehyde via a process of condensation was patented in Austria in 1911 by its developer, Dr Stiasny. The artificial tannin was called *neradol*, and was made under licence in Britain. It was expensive, with its cost doubling during the Great War.

The continuing development of machinery for leather production in this period had brought us to a place where, according to Adcock, that 'for practically every operation in the trade most of the machines require very little skill to work them, and can be operated by intelligent youths after a few weeks' experience.' (p53 of Adcock's book)

The hides were processed by being soaked in water, or a solution of borax in water, to clean them. If skins were obtained from the auction mart rather than directly from the butcher, they would have been salted to stop them rotting. This would require a longer soak to ensure that the salt was removed, as this would hinder the tanning process.

The next stage was the removal of hair. This was carried out with a variety of harmful and noxious substances such as lime, caustic soda, red arsenic sulphide, known as *realgar*, and sulphite of sodium. These chemicals were dangerous for the workers, as they dissolved keratinous matter such as hair and horn – and fingernails. After the hides had been soaked in the solution for between six days and a month, they were ready for scraping. Some scraping was still done by hand, with a traditional double handed blade, but many tanneries had introduced machinery by this period. The most popular was the *Leidgen*, as it could de-hair skins as well as a person employed to do so by hand at a quicker speed. The machine's use entailed setting the skin on a bed of felt, and feeding it through a roller. Spiral blades then removed the hairs quickly and efficiently.

After de-hairing, the hides were fleshed. That means they had scraps of flesh and fat scraped away. The 'fleshings', or 'spetches', were collected together in a weak lime solution, to stop them from rotting, until there was enough to send away to the glue factory to be boiled down into glue. In larger tanneries, glue was made on the same premises as a saleable by-product. After fleshing, the hides were de-limed. This was necessary to avoid the neutralisation of the acidic tanning liquor. In some factories, this still happened in large drums connected by pipes to a running water supply. In other, more 'modern' factories, science offered a different answer. Lime is alkali; an acid could be used to neutralise it. The skins were plunged into acid baths and great care needed to be taken to avoid the leather being over exposed and degraded. One would hope that the factory workers were protected too from this dangerous practice.

Incredibly, skins were still put in baths of a solution made with pigeon droppings for *bating*, before scudding. Calf skin was still *puered* with dog dung, and goat skin for kid leather or glacé kid (a kind of glazed, patented leather) needed the most puering of all, to make it soft and supple. However, science was beginning to offer alternatives to droppings and dung. *Oropon* was a mixture of trypsin, or pancreatin, and ammonium salts bulked out with sawdust as a carrier. The pancreatin was extracted from pig intestine, and had the effect of making the leather supple; the ammonium salts were used as a cleanser. This artificial bating material worked more quickly and was cleaner in use. Other chemicals being introduced in the US were *Erodin* and *Puerine*, a weak acid mixed with malt enzymes. The hides were scudded to remove fats and scum. Knives were still used for the scudding process. The scudding tool was a convex piece of either slate or vulcanite, a hard black rubber material, which was fitted into a handle for use. In some factories, skins were then *drenched*; treated with a solution of wheat bran or pea flour in water to further neutralise any remaining lime and to remove the last traces of scud. After rinsing, the skins would then be ready for tanning.

In the early part of the twentieth century, vegetable tanning using oak bark was still used in Britain, despite the drive for more artificial, efficient and cheaper solutions to be found via the laboratory. However, there was some move away from using plant materials in tanneries, instead using their extracts which were supplied by manufacturers solely engaged in their production. The extracts were dissolved in water at the tanneries to make the tanning solution.

Hides were *rounded* or trimmed, and then passed through a series of pits of tanning solution, starting weaker and then increasing in concentration. The hides were suspended on poles, attached by copper hooks or cords. Several different mechanical methods were used in different factories to move the hides through the liquor, such as a device that raised and lowered the skin to ensure equal coverage and uniformity of colour. In Britain hides were still mostly removed from pits and stacked to drain by hand at this time, however, which was expensive in terms of labour cost. Mechanisation had superseded human workforce in some areas where lighter grade leather was tanned using paddle or drum methods, which kept the skins and liquors moving to ensure even tanning.

Tanning was also done by 'mineral tannage', mainly using chrome, and carried out using mechanical means such as the drum tumbler or paddle-vat. Sometimes, combination tanning was employed. This could be a combination of chemical and vegetable tanning, or a combination of two chemical means of tanning. *Tragasol*, another chemist-driven development, was introduced in the rush to make tanning leather more efficient. This gummy product was extracted from vegetable seeds and used in the textiles industry for strengthening and sizing fabrics. It was found to increase the tensile strength of leather, and its addition to the tanning drum made consistent tanning easier to achieve. This saved time and labour costs. *Tragasol* increased the water resistance of leather massively. In tests, leather tanned with the addition of this substance was water resistant under six weeks of continuous exposure, compared to a few hours with ordinarily vegetable tanned leather.

The next step in the process was draining and drying the hides, usually in dark sheds, before finishing. The skins were then oiled with cod oil, linseed or mineral oil also being used. The oil was applied with a brush or swab and then the hide was hung up to dry again, until it was in a *sammed* condition – damp, but exuding no excess water. Then it would be *pinned* – scraped again to remove scum. In the early part of the twentieth century this was sometimes done by hand, with a knife, but mostly by machine. Machinery with rollers was used to clean and flatten the skins, which were then dried again, and sized with colourant such as annatto or turmeric, or chalk dissolved in white vinegar. The hides would then be polished with flannel.

During the Second World War the jerkins were still being made as standard issue. The Battle Jerkin was developed in 1942 by Colonel Rivers-McPherson. Still made from leather, this jerkin was a modified hunting vest. It had many pockets and was invaluable for assault troops despatched during the Normandy landings. In the US, the Shearling leather flying jackets and regulation leather boots were also part of the kit for every US airman. Leather was also used by the United States Air Force during the Second World War for an ingenious purpose: to make self-sealing leather fuel tanks for planes from chromium tanned leather.

Since the war effort was using so much of the leather being produced, there was less available on the home front. This was especially true for leather needed for boots, jackets and more. The government also wanted to release factory workers to fight, and wanted to utilise factory production for the war effort, so they put controls on production. Clothes rationing was announced by Oliver Lyttelton, President of the Board of Trade on 1 June 1941. This rationing scheme allocated items of clothing a 'points' value according to how much material was used, and how much labour the item took to produce. At first, people were allocated sixty-six points a year, but this fell to forty-eight in 1942, then to thirty-six by 1943. By 1945, the allocation was only twenty-four points for the year as materials became scarce and the workforce were depleted. When you consider that men's shoes were 'worth' nine points and women's shoes were 'worth' seven, new shoes were a luxury indeed.

Shoes were of course mended regularly and made to last for as long as possible. Iron studs were often hammered into the leather to reduce wear and many people had shoe repair kits and tools at home to prolong the life of their precious shoes. 'Utility' wear shoes were simple and plain, and used as little leather as possible, so that leather was not diverted from 'the war effort'.

After the war, once clothes rationing was lifted in March 1949, there were moves away from plain utility clothing and a return to high fashion. Styles for women became hyper-feminine, with nipped waists, full skirts and slim, gravity-defying stiletto heeled shoes. Slim heeled shoes had been around as a style since the 1930s, in 1954 Roger Vivier, a French designer working with Christian Dior introduced needle thin heeled shoes, popularly known as 'stilettos'. They had an internal steel or alloy stem to strengthen them. Other sources suggest that stiletto heels began with Salvatore Ferragamo, but whoever 'invented' them, they were a feat of engineering! As the shoes developed, injection moulding was used to encase metal posts in plastic to make them 'safe' to wear.

Leather jackets exploded onto the scene as a fashion item for young men in the 1950s thanks to Hollywood stars such as Marlon Brando wearing a Harley Davidson *Perfecto* jacket, designed by Irving Schott onscreen in *The Wild One* and James Dean in his leather jacketed 'bad boy' role in *Rebel Without a Cause*. Added to this, the rise of the phenomenon of the 'teenager' in the 1950s with money to spend on their own fashionable clothes aided in the rise of popularity of the leather jacket as a decorative rather than military or serviceable workwear item.

Historically, leather trousers had been worn by workmen and cowboys. These hardwearing trousers would last for decades – and would never be cleaned. Just let that sink in for a moment. In the second half of the twentieth century, leather trousers experienced something of a renaissance. Bikers would wear thick, leather trousers to protect themselves from spills onto the road, but it was in the entertainment industry that leather trousers really made their mark. In 1960, US singer Eddie Cochrane wiggled onto British television wearing leather trousers, and nothing like it had been seen before. Later in the 60s, Jim Morrison would pick up the leather trousers look and make it his own, with a sexy, bohemian style, and then in 1968, Elvis 'the pelvis' Presley swirled and gyrated his leather clad way into history with his 'comeback' outfit, clad from head to toe in black leather. Leather has been associated with rock stars ever since!

Iggy Pop had silver leather trousers and Marc Bolan of T Rex rocked in orange leatherwear in the 1970s – and so it went on. It's not just the boys who have made leatherwear iconic in the 70s; Joan Jett, Suzi Quatro and Chrissie Hynde made leather trousers the ultimate 'rock chick' look. Punks and New Romantics brought leather trousers out on to the high street, with Vivienne Westwood and Malcom McLaren dressing their entourage in strappy leather fetish and bondagewear: Siouxsie Sioux, Adam Ant, The Sex Pistols – and this inspired a generation of bright young things to don leather and make it their own.

Leather trousers are generally made from chrome tanned leather. Leather for trousers needs to be durable and robust, and the commonest skins used are cow hide, lamb, goatskin, and pig leather. Deerskin and even kangaroo skin have also been used widely.

So twentieth century leathercraft took us, in the west, through two World Wars, where leather was vital to the survival of troops and affected the 'war effort'. It then moved, via style icons of the screen and the music industry, into the realms of *street fashion*, accessible by all. Leather jackets and shoes became the part of every wardrobe. It was used for upholstery in homes and cars and this most ancient of materials is still widely used today.

Chapter 7

Modern Leathercraft

Today, there has been a welcome diversification in the leatherworking industry in Britain. Large scale production still exists, with leather being used in the automotive and aviation industries, for equestrian use, for furniture and fashion. The largest UK producers of leather is the Scottish Leather Group, which employs 550 people in the west of Scotland.

There has, however, been a decline in the actual *production* of leather in Britain, since its heyday in the 1900s, when they were around 4,000 working tanneries. By the 1980s, with overseas suppliers such as China and India dominating leather production at prices home producers could not match, the number of tanneries in the country dropped to 125. There are just twenty-three today. This is not just due to competition; UK producers face high production costs as effluent regulations become more stringent. Sadly, in developing countries there are often not such strong regulations and the environment suffers as it is polluted by chemicals – and so do the workers, who face many health problems as a result of working practices.

The UK continues to produce around 2.5 million hides a year. It seems counter-intuitive to think that 1.5 million of these are exported overseas, to China and Italy to be processed cheaply. Good quality leather produced in the UK is still in demand however by high end producers of leather goods.

Many modern techniques of production are surprisingly similar to historic methods. Once skins are flayed after slaughter, they are still preserved so that they can be shipped to tanneries, by using salt to preserve them for example, the same way it has happened for thousands of years. One major difference is that most leather today (around 90 per cent) is tanned with chromium, rather than vegetable tanning.

When a skin gets to the modern tannery, the first thing that happens is soaking. This is necessary for rehydration so a skin is ready to process. The soaking also helps to remove salt. Fleshing in commercial settings is carried out by machines today, rather than scraping knives, but some artisanal tanners will still do this.

Skins are de-haired with a solution of sodium sulphate and hydrated lime, and this process helps to hydrolyse fats for removal. After the skins are de-haired, they are de-limed with weak acid solutions. The skin is then chemically bated to clean the grain and make the resulting leather pliable. After bating, the skins are usually treated with sulphuric or formic acid to ready them to accept the tanning solution. At this stage skins may also be split and shaved. This entails splitting the hide longitudinally to create an upper grain and lower grain split. The shaving creates uniform skins, with a measurable consistency of form. Machines are used to carry out these operations.

Once the skins are ready to be tanned, they are immersed in solutions of chromium salts and occasionally in vegetable tannins. In recent times, glutaraldehyde has been introduced for tanning. This is seen as a more eco-friendly alternative to chromium salts which are pollutants. After tanning, the hides are neutralised to raise the pH, to make the hide ready to accept re-tanning and dyes. Re-tanning can change the colour of the hide and aid in the penetration of dyes. Chromium tanned leather is, in its natural form, a light blue and is dyed to obtain other colours.

After dyeing, the leather is finished with *fatliquors*. Chromium dyed leather is naturally hard and difficult to work, so it needs to be treated with emulsions of oil to make it flexible and soft. Once this has happened, the leather is dried. Modern techniques may include fast vacuum drying, where hides are dry in between two and ten minutes; alternatively, hides may be pegged onto frames and dried in heated tunnels for four to six hours. Once dry, the hides are buffed, polished and conditioned. They may also be milled. To finish, a variety of materials may be added. Resins and pigments, dyes, dullers and fillers may be used. This finishing process helps to hide any defects and create 'fashion' effects. The chemicals are added in layers, with machines spraying or rolling them on. Sometimes, finishes may be added by hand. Heated presses may then smooth the leather, or conversely add patterns to the leather surface. The leather is then ready to be despatched to make products such as shoes, clothing, upholstery and luggage.

Vegetable tanning is, however, on the upsurge in terms of small artisanal tanneries. This may be driven by the desire for more eco-friendly processes, and sometimes due to a need to create a high quality, workable leather. On a commercial basis in the United Kingdom, the only oak bark tannery still working is J.B. Baker and Co. Ltd. in Devon. Thomas Ware Ltd., in Bristol is still producing vegetable tanned leather 175 years after their first factory opened. But in smaller operations, vegetable tanning is growing as a practice, along with the growth and resurgence of natural dyeing techniques in textiles generally. The earthy tones that vegetable tanned leather develop make it perfect for artisans to create heirloom quality pieces of leathercraft. Vegetable tanned leather also develops an attractive aged quality and patina over time that chrome tanned leather does not. The spicy, almost horsey smell that we associate with leather is in fact the scent of vegetable tanned leather, and this is part of the pleasure that using and wearing leather brings. Vegetable tanned leather can (and has been found to) last for generations.

There have been many concerns about the chemicals used in leather production with chromium salts in terms of environmental impact and also in terms of health. On 1 May 2015, chromium was regulated within the EU by the REACH regulation. This restricts the levels of chromium allowed in leather products expected to be in close and regular contact with the skin, due to concerns in its role as a carcinogen. That would include watch straps, purses, wallets, gloves, shoes, clothing, dog leads, horse riding equipment, furniture, car seats and steering wheels. Chromium VI has been linked by some studies to the development of cancer, and can cause skin irritation, ulcers, sensitivity and dermatitis. This may well lead to a return to vegetable leather tanning, as it may be a safer option in terms of skin contact.

There are many artisanal grade leatherworking businesses emerging today. These are often micro-businesses, run by sole traders, and can be found throughout the United Kingdom. These crafters and artists draw on age old techniques for working leather, but reinterpret them for the modern day. Leather is used in everything from fashion – shoemaking, handbags and jackets – to steampunk accessories and historic re-enactment outfits. Live action replay (LARP) groups, and historic re-enactors often use traditionally leather crafted items of clothing and props, and epic films and television series such as *Vikings* and *The Tudors* have employed leather artisans to meticulously re-create historic items for the enjoyment of the viewing public.

These artisanal leather crafting businesses are keeping the hand-made heritage crafts alive. Leather items are cut, carved, tooled, punched and dyed before being moulded and sewn, using traditional and historic techniques, often redeveloped and adapted for the modern age. Many create, use and adapt historic or historically inspired patterns for shoes and clothing; others use traditional techniques to make newly designed leatherware. I have interviewed a selection of these talented and knowledgeable artisans who have kindly offered a view into their fascinating world.

Chapter 8

Artisan Interviews

The best way to find out about the modern artisans working in tanning and leatherwork today, is to ask them about their experiences, inspirations and artistic practices. With the advent of the Internet, it is easier than ever to find a window into the creative world of these artisans and to find out more.

These artists and crafters earn a living with their leathercraft. They have taken the leap into self-employment and sustain themselves and their families with their skill and artistry. I asked the artists a series of questions and encouraged them to describe their motivations, inspirations and goals for the future. They have taken traditional techniques and allowed them to evolve as they have explored their own ways of working with this versatile material.

You can find out more about each artist by following the links provided for their websites and social media. You can also buy their products directly, or even commission pieces yourself, and help to support the hand-made leather industry directly at source!

The Artisans

Jez Hunt, along with his brother **Mark** runs **Ancestor Leathercrafts**, from Newcastle-upon-Tyne. Originally from Wales, the brothers create fantastic leather pieces inspired by folklore, myths and legends, history and music. Jez worked as a leather merchant and maker, as well as a storyteller, costumier and creator of special effects and then in 2013 he decided to go it alone as a full-time leatherworker, and Ancestor Leathercrafts was born. From suits of armour to mystical masks; from pouches and bags to scabbards and arm bracers, their work is unique. Ancestor Leather specialises in painstakingly hand-carved and exquisitely painted pieces, often with a Celtic or Viking twist.

What first attracted you to your craft?
I've always made things. Both of my parents were great at making things (out of necessity initially) so I realised at an early age that everything was just made by people, so if you could work it out, you could make it too. Leather was always around as a kid, from my aunty working in a belt factory, to the tobacconists my dad went to that also sold belts and wallets.

I've worked in many materials over the years, and constantly drawn and painted, but it wasn't until I really started delving into the craft of leatherwork that I found a way of combining everything. I learn every day, with every project, and that's incredibly attractive and stimulating. Part of it is the variation in material, from soft lambskins for clothing, through to rawhide edging on shields, and the moulding of veg-tan leather for armour and masks.

Can you describe your journey into your craft?
I was always into history and fantasy and making things as a kid and I got into miniatures and role-playing games. At fourteen I discovered LARPing and that needed costume and armour, and I thought I'd have a go at making something. With my older brother doing most of the work, we made an aluminium helmet with leather inserts and that was the first leather protect I'd done. I carried on LARPing into my twenties, and moved up to Newcastle where there was a local leather merchants where I went to buy bits of leather and buckles for costumes I was making.

I saw a position going at the leather merchants and got the job. Over the next decade I learned a fair bit. Being surrounded by leather, and customers making things, and the other staff there meant I could get answers to questions I had and an endless stream of knowledge. I'd get back from work and make things, try out new ideas and different ways of doing things, honing my skills. It wasn't formal training, and certainly no qualifications, but a way of learning that suited me way more: a wealth of information, years of experience I could draw on, and lots of practical making in the evenings after work. I left the leather merchants to go self employed about four years ago and I'm still learning every day.

Do you have any inspirations or influences?
I'm inspired and influenced by way too many things – history, mythology and folklore, especially the cultures that have impacted Britain. The artistry, artefacts, landscapes and tales are an endless wellspring of ideas. I love the spirals and whorls of insular Celtic Iron Age art, the shapes of the megalithic cultures patterns, Anglo Saxon and Viking knotwork, Pictish animal carvings; this stuff seeps into your bones, and it finds its way out of my pencil and then onto leather. All the artists and writers I really love are the same; Tolkien, Brian Froud, Alan Lee, Robert Holdstock, John Howe, Alan Garner. A lot of these inspire TV and film, and they are always filled with leatherwork, be it belts and bags or armour.

What do you enjoy most about working with the materials that you choose to work with?
Leather is an incredible material. It's humanity's oldest fabric; we have spent all of history developing and refining it. The variation you can achieve is vast, from something incredibly soft and delicate through to something solid enough to bounce weapons off. Leatherwork is a strange mix that encompasses the practical building processes of something

like woodwork (I work alongside my brother, who I trained, and his background is as a joiner and it's got a strange overlap) through to the soft techniques of a seamstress, and the visual demands of being a painter.

Please describe the tools of your craft, and how you use them.
The tools that I use every day are pretty basic and you could fit the lot of them in half a small shoebox. I use a specialist knife, called a Clickers Knife, constantly. A sharp knife is the cornerstone of all leatherwork, and these have a forward hooked blade, that is quite stiff, but as sharp as a razor; it'll cope with almost anything. Then I use a pair of leather shears regularly. An awl is a must have; the design hasn't changed in thousands of years really. I use sturdy leather needles and linen thread to stitch most things with a traditional saddle stitch. I use a beveller to take the edge off leather after cutting it, giving it a more pleasing and long-lasting shape, and a tool called a groover to take a decorative channel out to stitch the leather in a neat line.

The item I use for all tooling and embossing on leather is a spoon-shaped modelling tool. I soak the veg tan leather, then use it to scribe and force down leather into the lines I want. Most people use a technique developed in the 1950s, involving a specialist swivel-knife and hundreds of stamps, but I find it a bit too restrictive for me. I use a series of punches and a hammer for larger holes and for applying rivets and press-studs. The only other tool I use regularly is a strap cutter, a wooden device that lets you cut perfect parallel edged strapping from hides. Dyeing leather I normally do with cloth rags or sponges, although I've recently got into applying them with an airbrush. It's not much at all, and you could get all of it for less than a hundred quid. We do have a sewing machine for sewing thinner leathers; it's a foot treadle old Singer, made on the banks of the Clyde in 1919 and it has a lovely sound. Our tools are mainly the same as people have used for millennia, all handheld.

Describe your business.

Ancestor Leathercrafts consists of myself and my older brother, who I trained up in leatherwork, which is good, as his stitching is much nicer than mine. We mostly make bags and pouches and armour, for all kinds of people, from film and TV, through to museums and re-enactors, and models – anyone really. We mostly work making commissions.

We've not done any courses as yet, although we plan to, but I got a reputation for being helpful, so I spend an hour or two every day answering questions and helping out leatherworkers I know, as well as starters in the craft. No point if you know this stuff to keeping it to yourself, knowledge should be shared.

My favourite makes are normally the one I have just finished. We've made a lot of nice bags, sturdy and practical, but with delicate design work on. Television work is always great fun, the demands for fine details are never as high as I put on myself, but it's generally a high-speed turnaround of a load of stuff. You get the big heap of leather needed, and you look at it, and know that you've got two weeks to turn that into a load of armour that millions of people might see.

Please describe a typical day.

The lovely thing about being self employed is I can work my own hours, so I don't do the 9-o'clock start thing, I generally start working at a much more civilised mid-day. The terrible thing about being self employed is I can never get away from work, and I tend to work until 2am most nights.

It suits me pretty well. I try and get admin out of the way, and then move onto most of the cutting and riveting I need to do for the day. Then it's onto the hours of stitching and dying. I tend to like doing fiddly and focused work at night time, as I find my concentration and patience is at its highest then, so that's when I do all my designing, tooling and painting work.

Long days, and pretty much the same all year round, and I always have music and documentaries and films on in the background, so it could be way worse!

What tradition 'heritage' methods do you use in your craft?
It's all heritage skills really. You could give a Roman or medieval leatherworker almost all of my tools and he'd use them in the same way. Nothing has really changed in the craft for centuries. Tanneries and dye makers are the real pioneers in the field, but that means something new may appear every five years rather than the relentless march in almost all other crafts and trades. A lot of leather tooling that is carried out was developed by an American chap called Al Stohlman, and it uses specific shaped stamps to tool leather, he developed this process in the 1950s, but even that was drawing upon older techniques. The way I tool leather involves pushing it down with a rounded tool, and it possibly dates back to the Stone Age. Most of the stitching we do is a thoroughly traditional 'saddle stitch', and it's pretty ubiquitous amongst leatherworkers and incredibly old. I was at Arbeia Roman Fort, in South Shields, doing a day on leatherwork and the museum staff brought out a bit of leatherwork that was excavated on the site. It was clearly a couple of bits of leather stitched together and another bit stitched over the top, but as the holes in it were the same size and shape made by modern awls, I could happily tell them that it was probably goatskin, and probably from a tent, and from the way the awl holes were in it (one line of neat same angled holes, one with the angles all over) that two people had stitched it; one who knew what he was doing, and one who wasn't so proficient. The process they used to stitch it is no different from what almost all leatherworkers still use.

How have you adapted heritage or historic methods for the modern day?
Most of the processes are the same as the way leather has always been worked; cutting out your shapes, tooling them or shaping them, dying

them, stitching or riveting them together. It was the same in the past. In some cases, other than a few cosmetic differences, a belt is no different now than it was a thousand years ago. People are pleasingly consistent with leather; we want attractive, well made things, the aesthetics may change slightly, but that's about it. When we are making bags, we are often asked to add a pocket big enough to add a smartphone in, or we may get asked to make a cover for a tablet, so it's the demands of technology wanting to be protected or carried about really.

When it comes to making armour, the demands of the human body are no different to those of the past. It has to encase the body, but not restrict its movements, and that has been the challenge of armour makers throughout the ages. As to whether people actually wore a lot of leather armour, well, you could write a whole contentious book on that. The making of armour, masks and some of our pouches involves a process called wet-moulding, where you immerse the veg-tan leather in warm water, then shape it (by hand or over a former of some kind), and as it dries it will hold that shape as long as the item is well waterproofed. The taste for this runs high at the moment; from historic film and TV fans wanting something similar, through LARPers cosplayers and re-enactors, but also for people who want something inspired by our past, but strong, well made and aesthetically pleasing.

Modern dyes are the real shift away for me. There's been a lot of developments in this in the past few years, and generally it's been in the right direction. I always used dyes in the standard way of applying them with a cloth (or sponge) but I have recently got hold of an airbrush, and this has made dyeing a lot more predictable, and a lot of the effects (such as fades in colours) a lot easier. When it comes to the more colourful decorations on pieces, I use totally up to the minute acrylics, thinned and mixed with a flexing medium, but applied with paintbrushes, so that's very much the best of the traditional and the contemporary really.

The real impact that technology has made, is in the people you can reach with this stuff. Social media has shrunk the world for artists and craftsmen of all kinds, and our Facebook page is followed by people from all over the world, which blows my mind. Twenty years ago, it would have been hard to get people from elsewhere in the country to see your work, never mind people in other parts of the world seeing it and buying it. Thanks to social media, we have sold things as far as Australia, and have returning customers in Germany and America.

What advice would you give someone starting out in your field?
Get making. It's the only way to learn.

YouTube has a load of info and tutorials, but go and find a leatherworker and talk to them. Then find another and you will find a different way to do the same thing, because leatherworkers are like that. We all develop our own way to do things. Try and soak all that up, you'll soon develop your own way too. Start with a simple project; make a belt. You'll use minimum tools and you can often buy pre-cut leather straps online, get a buckle to attach on it, get an awl, get some leather needles and some linen thread. If you hate it, you will have spent less money than you would on a half-decent belt and you will probably still have a reasonable belt.

Then move on to making a pouch, you'll use a different leather, maybe a couple more tools, but you'll be stitching more. Then make a bag or a mask and your skills will increase with each. Talk to as many leatherworkers as you can find; if you are lucky to have a leather merchants nearby, go in and ask some questions. Ask about courses. Like most crafts, it's a few pointers, then hours of making practice. Social media seems pretty good for things too; there is a host of great Facebook groups, with loads of people sharing tips and hints and showing off their work and asking questions. Be aware, though, that ten leatherworkers will have eight ways of doing things and they will all claim their way is the best way, and they are all correct.

If you enjoy leatherwork, it's enormously rewarding; you can spend a few hours and then you have a fully functional thing at the end of it; that's quite exciting, and also kind of addictive. Your hands will ache from stitching, your clothes and skin will end up covered in dye, you will stab and cut yourself a myriad of times, but you will be satisfied; and you will be doing and feeling the same thing as untold numbers of people have before you, as you will have become one stitch in the very long thread of leatherworkers reaching all the way back to the beginning of humanity.
https://www.facebook.com/AncestorLeathercrafts/
www.etsy.com/uk/shop/AncestorLeathercraft

Andy Bates runs **Phenix Studios** in Hexham, Northumberland. He is an expert in archaeological interpretation and reconstruction, using traditional materials and techniques. He has worked with museums, universities, theatre companies, production and television companies, The National Trust and English Heritage.

His philosophy: 'Ensuring the vitality of Living Heritage through our ability to Interpret, Create and Educate.'

What drew you to leathercraft in the first place?
I did English and archaeology at university and I've always made stuff and sort of tinkered with things. As part of my degree, I wrote a dissertation on Anglo-Saxon helmets and I thought I'm going to make a helmet and see how it goes. I made one and I really got on with the leather, and I did some of that re-enactment stuff back in the 80s and 90s. Ended up making my own stuff. I really got an appreciation for leather and the fact it's been a living material and the fact it's come from animals and that means it needs to be respected. There's a real relationship you can develop to it. So I started exploring that and I started off making historical pieces and I got the odd commission from

museums. I got to the point where I thought, I'm really enjoying this, maybe it's time I jump ship from the regular jobs and start doing this full time.

Did you do any sort of formalised training to start with or are you self-taught?
I tinkered with it for a few years making sort of re-enactment stuff, and then I thought I really need to get my skills sorted out so I went to find someone; there was a saddler, a guy called Maurice Savage down in County Durham. This was back in the early 90s. I worked alongside him and he got me to do stuff for a few months. I got some of the basics from him and apart from that, taught myself. I picked up every book I could find, anywhere, with making the historical stuff, quite often I got given an original piece to have a look at, to work out how it was made, how it was put together, what it was used for.

Have there been any people or historic periods that you've been influenced by?
There have been. Obviously in terms of sort of bags and designers I have been influenced, maybe subliminally. There's no one person but historically yes, there's been lots of influences. Originally it was early medieval stuff; really got into that. But it's actually been pretty much every period, because what I've found is when you are researching historical and archaeological things you can trace developments; you can trace people; you can trace people moving through this kind of continuum, over thousands and thousands of years, and using fundamentally the same techniques in different environments. You can – and this is going to sound esoteric – *feel* the person behind the work. You really get kind of inside them and start looking at it from their perspective and really you just feel them.

Is there a particular style you'd say that you've made your own?
I don't know to be honest, I think if there were it would probably be the kind of wet moulding process because I think I explored that to a very high degree, and made all kinds of stuff with that from building a complete suit of armour made to look like metal – but made in leather with tiny mouldings. We made three golden helmets for the *Beowulf* TV show out of leather. Each one had 280 separate pieces. Some of these were tiny panels which we worked with this moulding process.

I made some of the armour for a Discovery Channel programme called *The Bone Detective* at Bamburgh Castle. There were loads of bodies at Bamburgh, some of which had horrific wounds inflicted upon them, so we experimented with a sword maker from London, and a cuirass that I'd made earlier and it was just moulded leather, nothing more complicated than that and it was incredibly resistant to sword cuts. It was about 4mm thick. I think a lot of modern researchers have this habit of wanting to make things unnecessarily complicated, where actually if they could just reduce it down to its bare essentials. If it works, it's probably what they did.

What is the one thing that you'd made that you are most proud of?
A bag I made for Grayson Perry actually, not because of what he wanted, more because of the sort of technical problems that it presented. I think Grayson Perry's absolutely brilliant, I think his stuff's just stunning, he's an amazing man, but he's not a leather crafter so he sent me these illustrations of this bag and I'm thinking, how the hell would I shape that? I had to kind of mould it in these very specific panels for pleats, so I had to mould it and then cool the leather, and then bind the edges and incorporate a tangerine satin lining. And then it was moulding, I had to mould pimples onto the shape as well. I had to find materials to stuff parts of it, to give it the right degree of firmness and use materials that

to my knowledge haven't been used before. Ended up using the stuff that dentists take a mould of your teeth with to stuff it because you can pack it in to spaces and it's...

Quite turgid?
Yeah, that's a very good word, yes, very squidgy. It took me months to work it out and do it so it was, from a technical and creative point of view, probably the most satisfying. I had to literally invent new techniques so it was great to do that.

Do you have a typical day when you're working?
They vary from day to day, can be anything from the basic (admin) and getting emails out and stuff to sitting down and just making whatever it is that I'm currently working on. Or it might be research – maybe just reading or visiting museums and galleries. If it's working away like we did when we made armour for *The Iliad*, in Edinburgh last year, it entails travelling round the country, meeting actors, measuring actors and going to the theatre and working up there as well. On stage and off stage, having these great big butch actors waving these swords around coming up saying, 'It's chafing a bit up here', and we'll just shave a bit off.

How much teaching do you do?
A little bit at the moment but this year it's going to get very busy, because we're going to have the national leathercraft centre in Northampton and eventually, satellite premises around the country delivering these courses as well, so I'll be teaching people, but also teaching people to teach people, and assessing. We're doing that with NCFE. Teaching is one of the things I enjoy the most actually. People create this thing and they're just amazed by it, something they've created with their own hands and what have you, just has an amazingly beneficial effect, just, just, that's

just priceless. That's what it's about. You're also continuing the craft, you're implanting a lot of seeds as well.

You have these skills, this knowledge and this experience and you need to pass them on at some point, you're part of this continuum, I think; you're kind of a channel to channel towards other people and keep it going, it's not just manual skill either, it's sort of an attitude towards it.

How would you say you have adapted traditional methods?
I don't use sewing machines; everything's hand stitched. The tools I use are traditional, they've been around for centuries. The shape of the knife, the round knife that's the kind of traditional (saddlers) leatherworking tool, that shape of knife has been around since the early–middle of the Bronze Age, probably beyond. They're all very traditional. If I need a tool for a particular purpose and I have to make it, I tend to look to traditional tools for inspiration for doing it. They'll be in natural materials so when I was moulding these sets of armour, there's no particular tool, so I got some antlers and I polished them and rounded the ends off, got a nice curve, pressing into the leather, into the musculature of the armour. If I'm making things for museums which might be leather though, I work with other materials as well and I quite often use the tools from the period. I've got an old saddler's tack hammer with the handles a bit kind of warped, and it's really grubby with grease from all the hands and it's lovely thinking that people have used this for hundreds of years and I'm using it now.

What other materials do you work in?
Bone, antler, wood, metals sometimes, plant fibres…I kind of got into that a bit with the museum stuff. I don't do textiles, it's a bit too specialist, but what I find is a general repertoire of techniques, there's crossover, like a Venn diagram, and if you know something about one material, you've probably got an idea of how to go about working with another.

What advice would you give to somebody who starting out?
It'll be a lot quicker if you can find someone who can teach you rather than trying to teach yourself. Find a good teacher, stick at it, if you want to do it, just do it. Just go for it, it may take a while to get to that point but jump ship and do it. Nothing better, just make that decision and do it.

Tell me a little more about the book you are writing.
It's been great, I am trying to get in every technique that's been used for leather, ever, and describe it, keep it short and punchy, and at the same time it has to be interesting. Hopefully anybody can pick it up and go yeah, there's everything I need to know here. It's not the sort of text book that's saying, 'this is the way to do it and there's no other way to do it'. I've said right at the start, this is what I've done, this is how I do it, this is how I think it works. If you have another way of doing it, do that. Whatever works for you. It's due out this year.
https://www.facebook.com/AndyBatesLeatherStudio/
http://www.phenixstudios.com/

Angelique Taylor runs **The Raven's Daughter**, from Manchester. She makes bespoke and unique pieces such as wallets, belts, wrist bands, masks, dog collars and knife sheaths. Many of her pieces are 'wearable art' and feature accurate star maps of the constellations. She often uses crystals and animal totems in her work.

What first attracted you to your craft?
Having spent many years going to biker rallies I always liked to look at the leather goods stalls, I found however that they were all very directed towards a male market. I was always looking for something else but never found it.

Can you describe your journey into your craft?
After leaving university I had qualifications in art and design, design crafts and photography. I worked as a professional photographer and dabbled as a florist too so I was always looking for a creative outlet. I took a temp job in an office and I ended up being the operations manager but I hated it.

I woke up one morning and thought I just can't do this anymore. I sold everything I owned, jacked in the day job, cleared all debt, and for the first time in years I was free. At first this freedom thing was scary; I had a few hundred quid and no plan. Well, I was committed now so I left the city and went to live in Cornwall. On a day trip out to Padstow I happened upon Steve Brooks and his shop *Bag End Leather*. I was buzzing at everything he had for sale so I started asking questions and asked him to make me a cuff there. I did a sketch – nothing fancy – but the inspiration stuck. Leathercraft was for me. Money dwindling and living on packet noodles – but happier than I'd ever been. I knew this was what I was meant to be doing.

Do you have any inspirations or influences?
The themes in my work are influenced by my interests. I love Astronomy and can remember being a kid standing in my back garden with my Dad holding a planisphere and looking up at the constellations. I was fascinated at the beauty above me, the same as our predecessors would have been. I'm into mysticism and the occult, so you can find running themes in these subjects too appearing alongside nature or pop culture references. So, my influences are pretty eclectic! I find myself waking up with ideas in the middle of the night, to be swiftly scribbled down on paper or the back of my hand then upon waking find a load of backwards nonsense on my face!

What do you enjoy most about working with the materials that you choose to work with?

Leather as a medium is a tricky mistress. You can achieve the most amazing and beautiful results but it requires a lot of work and sometimes serendipity. Leather is unlike clay or canvas, because the exact same hide can tool and colour completely differently with each piece, as you're dealing with something that was a living creature. It can be frustrating especially when you've got customers waiting, but this is an art form and should be treated as such.

Please describe the tools of your craft, and how you use them.

The tools I use are pretty industry standard. I use a swivel knife to cut the design into the leather and then follow this with a beveller and hammer. Using backgrounder and matting stamps to add detail, I work in an intuitive way – basically making it up as I go along! So, I don't follow the traditional guidelines set down by the western tooling masters i.e. this tool for that etc. Why do things the way everyone else does? You'll just end up with a cookie cutter product.

Describe your business.

When I started out I wanted a name that reflected that I was female, as this industry traditionally is male dominated, so I chose **The Raven's Daughter**. I still get blokes saying, 'You made this?'

I make mainly small leather goods, but when time is permitting I like to make bags or basically anything with a tooled design. I mostly sell online, and every single sale is a buzz to me that someone out there in the world thinks my item is the one for them. To think I've sent items to far-flung places across the globe, that I have never been to, just blows my mind.

Please describe a typical day.
I do the admin first and get that out of the way; check overnight orders and reply to emails/queries etc. The rest of the day is spent making orders, creating new items or photographing them and updating my online store.

What tradition 'heritage' methods do you use in your craft?
The use of animal skins has been around since time as we know it began – not only in a utilitarian way but for decorative purpose too. The technique of scribing a design onto leather is not so far away now from how it first began. The leather I use for tooling is veg tanned, which has been tanned the same way using the bark and leaves of trees since ancient times. The process makes the leather more environmentally friendly and kind to the wearer's skin as it has no nasty chemicals so is a perfect choice for artisan leather goods.

How have you adapted heritage or historic methods for the modern day?
I produce my leatherwork using the same traditional techniques which our ancestors would have done, working by hand and hammering into the leather, with the addition of hand stitching. I find this is the only way to get the results and quality I desire in the end product.

What advice would you give someone starting out in your field?
When I first started out I found that people were not too helpful, and perversely this helped me because it made me find my own way. Today, **Tandy Leather** in Manchester are more than happy to help, and have a great informal drop-in where you can get help from experienced leathercrafters.

Join some forums. Leather worker.net is a great resource full of encouragement and help. Get some books, but mainly jump in and make mistakes – that's how you'll learn. Success is built on many, many, mistakes.

When you meet another leathercrafter in person don't be afraid to pick their brain. If we don't share this fascinating craft then it has no future. Find your own way; create the item you wanted but couldn't find in the first place and others will see it and want it.

Shop – www.TheRavensDaughter.com

Facebook - www.facebook.com/TheRavensDaughterLeather

Instagram - www.instagram.com/theravensdaughter

Twitter – twitter.com/Ravens_Daughter

Lacey Jean tans skins and hides using heritage and what she calls 'primitive' methods.

What first attracted you to your craft?

I found myself drawn to sheepskins and leather goods crafted by local artisans and farms but was discouraged to find that most were tanned using a chemical process. It seemed a shame that something as natural as an animal was being heavily processed after death to preserve it. I wanted to make something that was both practical, beautiful and with a resource that was underused or discarded. I have always longed to have a skill that was needed and necessary but not common. I found in our culture that we have an aversion to death and for many, the subject is taboo. I felt differently. I don't think of death as pain as I think many do. There is necessity in death. It is part of the cycle and even in it, there can be beauty and life. I see this pattern in nature and have found that many cultures that live close to the land and wild things understand this.

Can you describe your journey into your craft? How did you get started? For example, do you have particular training or qualifications, or are you self-taught?

I knew that native cultures have long been preserving skins and utilizing them for garments, warmth, décor, belts, boots, mattresses, cushions and beyond. I began reading and researching how it was done long ago. I was not surprised to find many articles that touted the longevity of leather garments and pelts that were traditionally tanned versus newer methods. It fanned the flame that I had begun to kindle for this craft and I have spent several years practising and often failing to hone this skill. As with many old methods, much of the process had to do with what was available in the region. Some cultures used bark, some brain and smoke, some salted, some left the skin to freeze in the elements, some chewed the hide to break it down, some strung the skin onto a frame. I realised that while I could spend hours mimicking a particular method, I would need to take stock of what was available to me, my own limitations and the climate I live in and make my own way.

Do you have any inspirations or influences? This could include particular artisans, periods in history etc.
I am heavily influenced by my ancestors. My heritage includes Norwegian, Irish and a smattering of Native American. Every culture has its own way of preserving the animals they raised or hunted to make the most of the resource, but I found inspiration from my own heritage. Many of my close relatives have raised sheep and I have a fondness for them. I now raise my own, a primitive breed from Iceland, and it is my vision to utilise every bit of each animal that I raise. Wool, meat, milk, horns, bone, skulls...etc. I will sometimes tan deerskin, rabbit and other critters, but sheep is my mainstay.

What do you enjoy most about working with the materials that you choose to work with?
It is hard work. It feels very primitive, very sacred and meditative. I feel I am connecting to ways that have long been forgotten, bringing them back to life as I feel I am giving new life to these skins. With care, primitive

tanned leathers and pelts can last hundreds of years. I ship my wares all over the world now and it feels very special to know that my craft is being enjoyed in the comfort of many homes around the world, hopefully offering warmth and comfort in the simplest way that humans have known for eons.

Please describe the tools of your craft, and how you use them.
I tell most people that my hands are my most used tool. They have become hardened, muscular and calloused. I am proud that my work is reflected in them. I also use old kitchen rocker knives. They are in a crescent shape and they allow me to clean the hides. I have built several wood frames on which I string the skins to stretch them. Most of the time I use the same kitchen rocker knife, sometimes I use a smooth hammer handle to push into the skin to stretch them. They are then smoked over a fire, washed and as they dry, I oil them and stretch them over a sharpened post that my husband built me for that very purpose.

Describe your business. What items do you make? Do you sell items – if so, what? Do you teach courses? Describe the thing you have made that has made you most proud.
I do indeed sell my wares. Quite by accident, to be honest. I began my craft to simply fill my home with the things I made and I considered it a hobby. Friends began requesting sheepskins and now I find myself with a waiting list that I have had to close as I have too many requests to fill. I have begun cleaning the skulls as well and have a waitlist for them now. My next venture will be making jewellery and buttons from the horns. I am most proud of some of the very first sheepskins I ever tanned, nearly four years ago now. They are in my living room, used every day as cushions. They have been carted outside to sit on during picnics and bonfires, they are used to add warmth to mattresses in the cold of winter. The cats and

dogs all love to curl up on them as well. They have been washed several times but retain their integrity and beauty. It feels so satisfying to know that my work has contributed to the aesthetic of my home as well as the quality of our days. And now the work being sold allows us more freedom as a family to pursue the things which we enjoy. Most of which is our farm. We are excited to see it grow as an outcome of my income.

You can explore Lacey Jean's work on Instagram

https://www.instagram.com/wildhair_homestead/

Chapter 9

Leathercrafting Methods and Materials

I f you have been inspired by reading about the work of the artisans featured in this book, you might want to go further and explore leather craft or even tanning methods yourself. Here is a directory of suppliers and course providers to help you to begin your creative tanning and leather crafting journey.

If you would like to have a go at leather crafting yourself, you may find these descriptions of methods and materials useful.

Carving

Leather is moistened or 'cased' with a moistened sponge and then compressed by carving to create an impression. If the leather is too dry, it will crack. If it is too wet, the impressions made will not hold.

Leather workers may use a pattern, traced onto the leather lightly with a stylus before carving. The leather is not cut when it is carved, but the pressure creates instead a decorative indentation in the leather that can also, if required, be painted or stained. A swivel knife is used like a pencil to outline and draw patterns deeply on the leather, up to half the depth of the leather itself.

Camouflage tools or 'cams' may also be used. These create an impression like a small scallop seashell. Cams are positioned and then tapped with a wooden mallet to create indentations to give a decorative three-dimensional textured effect. The tool is often tilted different ways to vary the effect created.

Other tools that may be used for the carving technique include a pear shader. These are used for contouring designs, and are held in place and tapped. Bevelers are used to raise designs by lowering the surrounding areas. They are used to compress one side of the cut (usually the outside edge) made by the swivel knife. They come in a variety of sizes and textures.

Veiners are used to create pattern and texture on scrolls, leaves and stems. These are available in a variety of sizes, curves and patterns. Seeders create round shapes, and are used to add definition such as circles at the centre of flowers, or to embellish designs. They once again come in a variety of sizes and may be smooth or textured. Backgrounders may be used to fill space, and increase definition. They come in a variety of shapes and patterns.

Decorative cuts may also be carefully made in the leather at this stage. Any minor mistakes may be addressed with a modelling tool. This spoon-shaped tool is run over the mistake with a light pressure to smooth and polish it out.

Moulding

When undyed vegetable tanned leather is moistened, the fibres expand and the leather can be stretched and moulded. For the moulding process, the leather is first soaked in warm water to make it pliable. How long it is left depends on how much moulding is required; the longer it is left, the stretchier it becomes; too wet though and it may become too flaccid to work properly. Leather can be submerged and left for a few minutes until no new air bubbles form, confirming saturation. The wet leather must be worked quickly before it starts to dry. It should be pressed and shaped around the mould with the hands, pushing and pulling the piece until the leatherworker is satisfied with the result. Thinner leather is easier to work than thicker leather, but thicker leather holds its shape better.

The leather should be left to dry completely on the mould. As the leather dries, it stiffens and holds the shape created.

Stamping

Specially shaped metal stamps are used to create an imprint on dampened vegetable tanned leather. A wooden or rayon mallet is used to tap the stamps so that the impression is made. The stamp marks stay in place once the leather dries. The leather is then rubbed with oils and fats to condition it and to help the impressions to stay in place.

Perforation

Punches may be used on leather to create holes or repeatedly to create latticework. The punches are held in place and tapped with a hammer to create holes.

Dyeing

Leather is often dyed with a variety of strong colours to create gorgeous effects. Alcohol-based dyes are absorbed quickly and easily by moistened leather, and strongly pigmented results are possible. These types of alcohol based dyes stiffen leather as it dries. Water based leather dyes are also available. These leave the leather soft and supple, but do not penetrate as deeply as the alcohol based dyes. All leather dyes should be used in a well-ventilated space to guard against any harmful fumes that may be produced. Dye may be applied with a brush, sprayer, sponges or wool daubers. Several coats may be used to deepen of even mix effects. Stains may also be used to add definition to patterns that have been created by other means.

Leather may be dyed using a traditional solution called *vinegaroon*, or vinegar black. It creates a black permanent dye. This is made by adding rusty objects to warmed white vinegar. Nails, screws, nuts, bolts

– anything rusty. The rust, which is caused when iron oxidises in the air to create iron oxide, combines with the vinegar, which is acetic acid. This creates a substance called ferric acetate, which will dye the leather. The mixture should be left in a warm place until the iron dissolves – but it should not have a lid placed upon it during the process as the reaction gives off gases that will cause the container to pop. A warm shed in summer would be a good place to create this solution. The *vinegaroon* is ready when the vinegar smell is gone. Rusty iron can be added to the solution until no more dissolves.

Once the solution is ready, it can be filtered through kitchen roll or a coffee filter to remove solids. Prepare your leather by soaking it in strong black tea – it needs the tannins in the tea to react with the *vinegaroon* to dye the leather. Professional tanners would use a solution made with crushed oak bark or logwood chips to provide tannin. The leather item should then be soaked in the *vinegaroon* for up to thirty minutes. Once removed from the solution, the acid should be neutralised to prevent later deterioration of the leather. This can be achieved by dissolving baking soda in water and saturating the leather in the solution.

Painting

Paint, such as acrylic or latex paint can be used to decorate leather items. Unlike dye, that seeps into the leather, paint lays on the surface. This means that on a particularly flexible piece such as a belt, paint can flake unless flexible latex-based paint is used.

Pyrography

Pyrography uses a heated needle point to draw designs. This can be used on leather as well as on wood surfaces. The heat darkens the leather where the point touches, and it is possible to create complex designs and pictures in this way.

Materials

There are several different types of leather. **Full-grain** leather is hide that has not been treated to remove imperfections or faults on the surface of the leather. It is strong and breathable, and develops a beautiful patina over years of use. Full grain leather is a high quality product that is used for footwear, high quality jackets and upholstery.

Top grain leather is the type of leather used for most high end and expensive leather products. Its surface is generally sanded and it has had a coat added to the surface. It is more stainproof than full grain leather, but does not develop a patina over time. **Corrected grain** leather is cheaper and has had faults and imperfections sanded off and an artificial grain embossed on the surface. It is usually dyed, as this also helps to cover imperfections. **Split leather** is the grade of leather left behind when a hide has been split to remove the top grain. An artificial layer can be added and this is then embossed with a leather grain. Suede, which is fluffy on both sides can also be made this way.

Nubuck is top grain cattle hide with a velvety surface, created by sanding or buffing. **Russia** leather high quality bark tanned cow hide, treated in the traditional way where birch oil is applied after tanning. It is highly water resistant.

Exotic leathers are gaining in popularity. Crocodile and reptile leather such as snakeskin and lizard skin has been used since the Victorian era. Victorian and Edwardian handbags and purses often celebrated the 'exotic' nature of the skins, keeping the original texture and natural colour shades. Some of these bags included gruesome taxidermied elements such as the head or paws of the animal. American alligators from Louisiana were harvested in great numbers in the early 1800s and the skins were used to make boots, bags and saddles. During the American Civil War, alligator skins were used to make boots and saddles for Confederate soldiers. By the mid twentieth century, the alligators were endangered and a programme of farming and breeding began. A proportion of alligators bred (between 14 and 17 per cent) were released back into the swamps, which repopulated. The alligator was removed from the endangered list in 1987.

Alligator skin leather is soft and flexible. Once tanned, the skin is supple and bends without creasing. It is made with both matte and glossy glazed finishes. The skins are large, and can be used to make upholstered pieces and clothing, but they are expensive.

Fish leather, with its gorgeous scale patterns, is used for making shoes, bags and journal covers. It has about the same strength in application as sheep skin. A wide variety of fish skins have been made into leather. It is tanned in the same way as mammalian leather and the pattern and texture on the skins is made by the 'scale pocket' that remains after the scales have been removed.

Salmon creates a beautiful, strong, finely scaled leather that looks a little like snakeskin. Cod skin is similar but its texture is more variable and can sometimes be rough. Tilapia, or Cichlid Fish is a popular fish leather with almost cartoonishly perfect scale patterns. Nile Perch is similar, but with larger scales and a honeycomb effect texture. Wolffish is smooth and scale free, and patterned with spots and stripes. Eel skin is also scale-less and somewhat shiny. Stingray leather, known as shagreen, is tough and durable with a bumpy surface. It is used for motor racing gloves, where its rough surface makes a safe surface that is hard to wear through even in the event of an accident. It is also used traditionally for the handles of Japanese *katanas*. The skin is covered in minute calcium rich bubbles that make it able to resist scratching and puncturing. It is also difficult to tear as it has fibres that run in different, random directions. It is stain and water resistant and is also hard to cut as a result of these qualities, so it takes longer to create stingray leather products.

Arapaima, a freshwater fish from the Amazon, is also used for leather making. It is one of the world's largest freshwater fish, and has a unique two–layer skin. This acts like armour to protect the fish in the wild. The top layer is tough, with scales that resist puncture and the bottom layer is soft like a sort of gel. This quality resists and absorbs impact. As a leather, tanned Arapaima is hardwearing and resistant to scrapes and scratches, but it is highly flexible. The skin is expensive, but comes in large panels due to the size of the fish. Carp leather has a large scale pattern and Sea Bass skin is also made into leather which is used for accessories and footwear.

Shark skin is also used to make leather. It is covered in fine scales, called denticles or dermal scales which are like minute hard teeth, which can bristle like fur. It is tough and has a tensile strength five times that of cow hide, but it is difficult to work. At one point it was used as a type of sandpaper and to cap shoes to prevent wear. Shark leather is used to create handbags, wallets, gloves, jackets and upholstery. The skins of Tiger, Lemon, Shortfin Mako, Porbeagle, Nurse, Bull, Hammerhead and Dusky sharks are all used to make leather. The finished product is waterproof and supple. In Morocco, shark leather is used in book binding and to cover jewel boxes. In France, Louis XV had a master leatherworker in his employ, called Jean-Claude Galluchat, who popularised shark leather or *shagreen*. This luxury leather became popular again in the Art Deco period in the 1930s for high end goods such as jewellery cases, bags, make up cases and compacts. Before fish leather was popular, fish skin was a waste product that was often thrown back into the sea by fisheries and this had the potential to pollute the water.

Bird leather is also becoming popular. Ostrich feathers have been used for centuries and the birds were farmed for their feathers in the nineteenth century. More recently, ostriches have been farmed for meat and their skin has been made into leather as a by-product. Ostrich leather is used for shoes, accessories, designer clothing, and upholstery. The leather has characteristic raised bumps as a result of the large follicles on the skin where the feathers grew.

Suppliers, Training Courses and Books

Directory of Suppliers

These suppliers can provide you with everything you need, from tools and fastenings to the finest leather and skins.

Leather and leatherworking supplies and tools, Newcastle upon Tyne http://www.leprevo.co.uk/

Leather working Tools, Supplies, Worcestershire http://www.bowstock.co.uk/

Tanners, dyers and finishers, Leeds http://www.cfstead.com/

Leather and Suede, Glasgow http://www.clydeleather.co.uk/

Goatskin and calfskin bookbinding leathers, Northampton http://www.harmatan.co.uk/

Leather, tools, supplies, Devon http://www.artisanleather.co.uk/

Stamps http://www.artisans.co.uk/

Leather, tools, supplies, https://www.tandyleather.eu/en/

Leather, supplies, Somerset https://www.pittards.com/

Leather, Northampton http://www.aacrack.co.uk/

Leather, West Yorkshire http://www.jwoodleathers.co.uk/

Leather, fasteners, thread, Cheshire http://abbeyengland.com/

Leather, Northampton http://www.metropolitanleather.com/

Tools, supplies, Lytham St Annes http://www.hedgehogleather.co.uk/

White oak bark for tanning (US Supplier) https://www.etsy.com/uk/shop/ScentsibleCrafts

Tanning Supplies, Conway http://www.snowdoniasupplies.co.uk/

Tannery http://www.cfstead.com/

Vegetable tanned leather, Bristol http://thomasware.co.uk/

Oak Bark tanned leather, Devon http://www.jfjbaker.co.uk/

Leather; specialising in vegetable tanned leather finishing since 1919, London http://www.metropolitanleather.com

Everything from leather to dyes and tools, Cheshire http://jtbatchelor.co.uk/

If reading this book has whetted your appetite for having a go at leatherwork yourself, there are many courses available across Britain. Here is a list to get you started.

Training Courses
Pembrokeshire, West Wales https://leathercoursesbritain.com/

Kent http://www.rosannaclare.co.uk/

Shropshire http://www.saddlerycourses.com/

Moretonhampstead http://www.greenshoes.co.uk/

Gloucestershire https://www.leathercourses.co.uk/

Staffordshire http://www.armitageleather.com

Dartington, Totnes https://www.tannerbates.co.uk/

Dumfriesshire http://www.half-goat-leatherwork.co.uk/

Ripon, North Yorkshire http://www.thewildmanbushcraftcompany.com

Frome http://www.bespokeleather.co.uk/

Herefordshire http://www.williamshandmade.com

London http://www.theshoemakingschool.co.uk/

Saddleworth http://www.diamondawl.co.uk/

Derbyshire https://judicook.co.uk/

Bishop Aukland http://www.evancliffeleather.co.uk/training-workshops

Lincolnshire http://www.lincolncastle.com

East Ayrshire http://www.a-finlay-primitive-crafts.co.uk

Cumbria http://www.layapoint.com/courses/shamanic-drum-birthing-workshop/

Leather Conservation Centre http://www.leatherconservation.org/education/

Useful Books

Should you be interested in learning more about the practical aspects of leatherwork, and trying some techniques yourself, here is a list of useful and interesting books about tanning and leatherwork.

Richards, Matt *Deerskins into Buckskins: How to tan with brains, soap or eggs* (Backcountry Publications, 2004 ISBN 0965872472)

Hobson, Phyllis *Tan Your Hide* (Storey Books, 2000 ISBN 0882661019)

Michael, Valerie *The Leather Working Handbook* (Cassell, 2006 ISBN 1844034747)

West, Geoffrey *Leather work: A Manual of Techniques* (The Crowood Press, 2005 ISBN 1861267428)

Guild of Master Craftsmen *Leathercraft: Inspirational Projects for You and Your Home* (Guild of Master Craftsman Publications Ltd., 2016 ISBN 1784941727)

Ubach, Thomas *The Art and Craft of Leather: Leather working Tools and Techniques Explained in Detail* (Barron's Educational Series, 2008 ISBN 0764160818)

Ingrams, Otis *Leather works: Traditional Craft for Modern Living* (Jacqui Small LLP, 2017 ISBN 191112725X)

Irish, Laura *Art of Leather Burning: Step by Step Pyrography Techniques* (Dover, 2017 ISBN 0486809420)

Salaman, R.A. *Dictionary of Leather Working Tools c. 1700–1950 and the Tools of Allied Trades* (Astragal Press, 1996 ISBN 18793357270)

Grant, Bruce *Leather Braiding* (Schiffer Publishing Ltd., 2010 ISBN 087033039X)

Stohlman, Al *Leathercraft Tools: How to Use Them; How to Sharpen Them* (Tandy, 1984 ISBN 1892214903)

Pogson, Katherine *How to Work with Leather: Easy Techniques and Over 20 Great Projects* (Collins and Brown, 2016 1911163264)

Useful Websites

Museum of London – a generally excellent resource for the curious, and this section is a fascinating study of a sixteenth century jerkin https://www.museumoflondon.org.uk/discover/leather-jerkin-well-examined

Archaeological Leather Group – A collection of knowledgeable archaeologists, historians scholars, conservators, scientists and leatherworkers who work to promote the study of historic leather and the history of leathercraft

http://www.archleathgrp.org.uk/

Imolc Museum of Leathercraft, Northampton

This museum collects, preserves and makes publicly accessible historic leather and fur articles. It has, and is building, a collection of documents and information for the study of leather craft, and aims to support present and emerging leather craft professionals.

Contact Philip Warner, Collections and Engagement Officer info@ imolc.com

http://www.imolc.com/

Traditional hand-made shoes

http://www.johnlobbltd.co.uk/

The techniques used by modern leatherworkers have been developed over the course of centuries of leather craft. This truly makes it a heritage craft, with techniques built and developed on historic practices.

http://www.vikingleathercrafts.com

Viking era replica leathercraft/shoes

Index